INSTANT IMPACT

EFFECTIVE LEADERSHIP COACHING FOR TRANSFORMATIONAL LEADERS

Luke Salway - MCC
Cristy Aphimonthol - MCC

BALBOA.PRESS
A DIVISION OF HAY HOUSE

Copyright © 2024 Luke Salway - MCC & Cristy Aphimonthol - MCC.

All rights reserved. No part of this book may be used or reproduced by any means, graphic, electronic, or mechanical, including photocopying, recording, taping or by any information storage retrieval system without the written permission of the author except in the case of brief quotations embodied in critical articles and reviews.

Balboa Press books may be ordered through booksellers or by contacting:

Balboa Press
A Division of Hay House
1663 Liberty Drive
Bloomington, IN 47403
www.balboapress.com.au
AU TFN: 1 800 844 925 (Toll Free inside Australia)
AU Local: (02) 8310 7086 (+61 2 8310 7086 from outside Australia)

Because of the dynamic nature of the Internet, any web addresses or links contained in this book may have changed since publication and may no longer be valid. The views expressed in this work are solely those of the author and do not necessarily reflect the views of the publisher, and the publisher hereby disclaims any responsibility for them.

The author of this book does not dispense medical advice or prescribe the use of any technique as a form of treatment for physical, emotional, or medical problems without the advice of a physician, either directly or indirectly. The intent of the author is only to offer information of a general nature to help you in your quest for emotional and spiritual well-being. In the event you use any of the information in this book for yourself, which is your constitutional right, the author and the publisher assume no responsibility for your actions.

Interior Image Credit: Adisak Thongprond

Any people depicted in stock imagery provided by Getty Images are models, and such images are being used for illustrative purposes only. Certain stock imagery © Getty Images.

Print information available on the last page.

ISBN: 979-8-7652-0044-5 (sc)
ISBN: 979-8-7652-0045-2 (e)

Balboa Press rev. date: 09/27/2024

Endorsements

"Luke Salway's *Instant Impact* is an outstanding guide for leaders aiming to make a significant impact in their organizations. With decades of experience, Luke offers practical, actionable strategies through the POW Coaching Model. This book is filled with clear methods to foster engagement, empowerment, and high performance within teams. It's a must-read for any leader or coach looking to inspire and drive impactful change."

Dr. Marshall Goldsmith
Dr. Marshall Goldsmith is the *Thinkers50* #1 Executive Coach and New York Times bestselling author of *The Earned Life*, *Triggers*, and *What Got You Here Won't Get You There*.

"**INSTANT IMPACT: Effective Leadership Coaching for Transformational Leaders**" is an invaluable companion for those aiming to quickly ignite collective intelligence within their teams. Written by renowned and accomplished coaches and trainers, this book stands out for its practicality and ease of reading. It provides numerous examples of brief coaching conversations, empowering you to immediately create more value in your interactions. Highly recommended for leaders, executives, HR professionals, and coaches!"

Jean-Francois Cousin, MCC
Global Executive and Team Coach, Speaker and Author, Chairman, Global Board, International Coaching Federation, 2019

"INSTANT IMPACT" introduces the POW Coaching Model, a framework for conducting effective twenty-minute coaching conversations for busy leaders. You'll discover what it means to create a balanced Leadership Development Matrix, and a redefinition of SMART goals to focus on solutions rather than problems. The book is filled with practical examples of workplace coaching conversations, and it addresses resistance to leadership coaching by offering a troubleshooting guide for coaching challenges.

Also included are templates, frameworks, and lifetime access to video tutorials and demonstrations, aiding full implementation of the techniques. This book is essential for anyone looking to enhance their leadership skills."

Howard Bryant, Chairman, Retail Asia Limited

"Over the years I've worked with Luke on organizational change and alignment. Luke was involved in helping myself and my team through different changes in our business, in a one-on-one setting and with team coaching and workshop sessions to a wider group. These sessions were always well received and had the desired impact of the team questioning **what** and **how** things can be improved. Lukes enthusiasm for helping to improve teams is outstanding, and the tools and techniques I've witnessed over the years have been beautifully distilled into his book Instant Impact. A must read for Leaders passionate about developing teams."

Bob Waller, Managing Director, Global Food Ingredients Manufacturer

"Master Coaches Luke and Cristy have crafted a masterpiece for coaches, executives, and anyone interested in impactful, organic coaching conversations that drive meaningful change. They provide accessible, straightforward yet powerful tools to facilitate success."

Timothy Grubbs, MBA, PCC, Managing Partner, CedarStone Coaching

"Having worked with Luke on a multitude of programs, I can say "Instant Impact" puts on paper everything I have seen Luke achieve with our clients. He brings a wealth of experience and knowhow to the coaching conversation. Luke grabs learners' attention and leads them to a higher level of understanding, all while maintaining energy, passion and fun. It is one of the best ways to learn – with a smile on your face. I can recommend "Instant Impact" to any leader aiming to remove the mystery from personal leadership and adopt some commonsense coaching tools, to better support the growth of those they lead."

Scott McCormack, Senior Director, GP Strategies

"As someone who wants to continue evolving and is passionate in unlocking people's potential, this book provides hands-on and impactful framework for conversational coaching. Common resistance to coaching including ego and lack of rapport was addressed together with the practical strategies to overcome them.

Instant Impact is a must-have book for any leaders who are committed to promoting coaching culture that drives impactful results for the organization. It provides leaders skills for easy coaching talks that motivate/inspire the teams and enable them to be more engaged and productive"

Antiek Wahyu, VP People, BlueScope

"Having known Luke Salway for many years, I can confirm that he truly walks the talk—putting into practice everything he teaches. *Instant Impact* is a must-read for leaders who want to implement real, transformative change. Drawing on his extensive experience, Luke provides a clear and effective framework with the POW Coaching Model, making it accessible and actionable for leaders at any level. This book is a testament to his dedication to empowering others and creating lasting impact."

Stuart Wilson, Founder of Breath Inspired

"**Instant Impact** is a must read for leaders at all levels that offers practical, actionable and reality-based strategies and techniques for today's leader to achieve success in any environment. Luke Salway is a tier 1 leader and leadership coach who for decades has inspired thousands to improve and add to their leadership toolbox resulting in unparalleled outcomes across hundreds of local, national and international organizations. I have collaborated with Luke for many years, have attended his seminars, and have utilized his proven techniques in my daily life, military conflict environments, private sector and federal government's that have resulted in enormous success. Simply put, if you are looking to improve yourself, your leadership, your relationships, your communications and enjoy a life full of success than look no further than Instant Impact – take the teachings and soar…."

Bernie Derible, Deputy Minister and Commissioner Emergency Management Ontario, Canada
Colonel (retired)

"Having had the pleasure of working with Luke in one of our talent development programs, I've seen firsthand the incredible impact he has on our coachees. Luke's sessions are nothing short of engaging and transformative—he connects with learners in a way that is both energizing and deeply impactful. *Instant Impact* captures the essence of Luke's dynamic coaching style, translating his larger-than-life presence and practical wisdom into a guide that's as engaging as it is effective. I have no doubt that this book will resonate with leaders looking to elevate their coaching skills and inspire those they lead, just as Luke has done for us."

Janil Jose Samson, Group Director of Organizational Capability, Minor Group

"Luke Salway's *Instant Impact* truly captures the essence of his transformational coaching style. As someone who has had the privilege of being coached by Luke and having my senior leadership team trained by him, I've seen firsthand the remarkable difference he makes. His unique ability to distill complex leadership concepts into practical, actionable strategies empowers leaders to elevate not only their own performance but that of their teams as well. Luke's energy, clarity, and passion for growth have inspired a lasting impact on our organization. He does it all with a big smile, making the learning journey engaging and enjoyable. I strongly recommend *Instant Impact* to any leader who is serious about developing their leadership skills and fostering high-performing teams. It's a must-read for those seeking real, sustainable change."

Thomas Tait, COO South-East Asia, Narai Hospitality Group

Contents

Chapter 1	Introduction	1
Chapter 2	Definitions	4
Chapter 3	What is Leadership Coaching and its Benefits	10
Chapter 4	Overcoming the three biggest obstacles to resistance	26
Chapter 5	Correct SMART Goal Setting – We've been doing it wrong	40
Chapter 6	POW Coaching Model Overview	68
Chapter 7	P = Problem. Clearly identifying the Problem/Challenge	73
Chapter 8	O = Outcome. Shifting focus towards a crystal-clear SMART Goal	83
Chapter 9	W = Way Forward. What are the very next physical actions	89
Chapter 10	Practical POW Coaching Applications	102
Chapter 11	Troubleshooting Your Coaching Conversations	112
Chapter 12	Acknowledgments	123

Chapter 1
Introduction

The purpose of **INSTANT IMPACT: Effective Leadership Coaching for Transformational Leaders** is to support you with proven, practical strategies, for short, sharp, and structured Coaching Conversations, that create impactful results for individuals and teams. The lessons within this book gives you a framework for the power of 'conversational coaching', which is designed to empower each member of your team, to be their best, in a more organic and natural style. Imagine being able to conduct effortless coaching conversations that motivate, inspire and positively impact others to solve their own problems, as you casually converse at the water cooler or coffee machine?!

"But we don't have time to Coach" can be heard echoing through the halls of many an organization, from the cynical mouths of both Coach and Coachee. That stops now!!

In your hands, you hold a framework for effective and efficient Leadership Coaching Conversations, that can be facilitated in twenty minutes or less.

Chances are you're a Leader or Senior Executive, HR/L&D professional, or anyone passionate to help others grow. This Coaching framework supports and aligns with your existing Leadership skills, and applies to any industry, of any size, in any part of the world.

Coaching is the evolution of Leadership, and you are now at the forefront of accelerated results, people empowerment, and Instant Impact.

As a Master Facilitator, an MCC certified ICF Coach, NLP Trainer, and as a Leader for more than twenty years, I've had the opportunity to work with thousands of clients 1-on-1 and have been blessed to work with hundreds of multi-national organizations, employing thousands of Leaders, helping them all achieve their goals faster, through the application of Leadership Coaching principles. This book has been ten years in the making, as together with my partner and co-author Cristy Aphimonthol, MCC, we've accumulated more than twenty thousand client-facing hours and have extracted the best practices to save you time, to achieve faster results.

One of the fundamental leadership coaching tools you will discover in this book is the POW Coaching Model. POW is an acronym for the following:

P = Problem/Challenge
O = Outcome
W = Way Forward

This seemingly simple yet powerful framework has helped hundreds of forward-thinking companies to Create and Implement a sustainable Coaching Culture, that really works.

The POW Coaching Model forms part of our larger ICF accredited Leadership Coaching Certification Program, which is available worldwide as face-to-face training or virtually. The ICF, also known as the International Coaching Federation, is the world's largest coaching authority. At 65 hours duration, this advanced Coaching program is not always practical for busy Leaders to attend, so for organizations that are serious about the implementation of a

Coaching Culture, we offer shorter programs of twelve to twenty hours, to support the application of these proven coaching principles.

Together with this book, you have access to online learning videos, that you can watch, with each chapter. Conveniently split into bit-sized modules of twenty to forty minutes, you can watch all the videos first, or with each chapter as you progress. Simply scan the QR codes and the end of each chapter.

We hope you enjoy INSTANT IMPACT: Effective Leadership Coaching for Transformational Leaders, and more importantly, we hope it helps you, and your teams, solve more problems and achieve MORE goals.

Chapter 2
Definitions

"Clarity precedes success."
— Robin Sharma

Before we dive fully into *Instant Impact*, let's clear the air with some definitions that will help demystify the language of coaching, to create greater clarity.

a. **Coaching** – The ICF definition of coaching, which honours the co-creation process:

"Partnering with clients/coachees in a thought-provoking and creative process that inspires them to maximize their personal and professional potential."

To simplify this even further, you can think of coaching as...

"More asking and listening, less telling"

In other words, a Coach will not tell you what to do. A Coach will not give you an action plan. A Coach will not give you options. A Coach will ask you questions, to help you to discover the solution for yourself. A Coach will do less talking and more listening. This is a great way to empower others, unleash higher potential, and build confidence in your coachee or clients. Coaching alone does however have some limitations. To be a truly effective Leader involves a combination of Coaching, Mentoring, Training and some Telling, to get the best results. We'll expand more on this when we discover the Leadership Development Matrix.

b. **Standards of Professional Coaching** – as a certified ICF Coach and ICF Coach Training provider, it is important to acknowledge the professional standards of Coaching, with which INSTANT IMPACT and the coaching models within, are aligned. In summary, a professional Coach will:

   – Ensure that the details of every coaching conversation remain **confidential**

   – Refrain from **TELLING** the Coachee what to do. That's not coaching and is more aligned with Mentoring, Consulting, or general Leadership practice. We'll expand more on this point throughout the book

   – Remain professional at all times, by honouring the Coachee as whole, creative and resourceful

   – Respect the clients' experiences, personality, culture, values, beliefs, and religion

   – Refrain from judgment or behaviour that would be deemed inappropriate, such as sexual advances, physical contact, sarcasm, etc

   – Create a safe environment in which the Coachee can fully express themselves. Ensure an environment of Psychological Safety, where your coachee feels safe to speak up with ideas, questions, concerns, or mistakes, without fear of judgment, humiliation, or blame

c. **Mentoring** – According to google (so it must be true) the definition of Mentoring is "A professional relationship in which an experienced person (the **mentor**) assists another (the **mentee**) in developing specific skills and knowledge that will enhance their professional and personal growth"

In other words, the Mentor will guide the lesser experienced mentee to achieve and accelerate their competence, in a specific skill.

The best Mentoring practice is a combination of telling, showing, guiding, and asking questions. The Mentor should ideally be considered as a role model, in that specific area of expertise. The Mentor does NOT have to be an expert in every single area of Leadership. A Mentor will provide a road map or recipe for success, which when followed, will help others accelerate their success, in a shorter period. Mentoring is an essential factor to consider when implementing a Coaching Culture.

d. **Training** – "the action of teaching a person a particular skill or type of behaviour".

The Trainer will do a lot more speaking than listening, which is the opposite of Coaching. The trainer will often teach specific skills, tools and techniques, to improve the competence of the audience. It can be hard skills, such as using a piece of software, operating machinery, safety protocols, and a myriad of other 'technical' types of education. Training can also include soft skills, such as specific leadership tools, communication, Emotional Intelligence, conflict resolution, etc.

Training is not much different from traditional teaching that you experienced back in school. The main difference is that with training, there is usually an element of practice, role play, or simulation, to help participants understand the concept being taught. Without this kind of application, the training can be quite dull and not very effective.

e. **Facilitation** – this is my passion. I define facilitation as a combination of Training, Coaching and Mentoring, and as a result, the students and participants have a much higher engagement, as you touch on each of the preferred learning styles of the audience, help them accelerate their development, and address specific needs that the audience have.

Google definition of a facilitator (one who facilitates) is as follows:

"A facilitator often helps a group of people to understand their common objectives and assists them to plan how to achieve these objectives: in doing so, the facilitator remains "neutral", meaning he/she does not take a particular position in the discussion."

Within an organization, Facilitation works perfectly in any problem-solving type of scenario, brainstorming and group coaching. We'll expand on this a little more shortly.

f. **Goal** – "the object of a person's ambition or effort: an aim or desired result.".

A goal is simply the final destination. Something your coachee would like to achieve. This will also be referred to as an **outcome** throughout the book.

g. **Coach** – typically, most people associate the word coach to a "sports coach" where the definition would be:

"Someone whose job is to teach people to improve at a sport, skill, or school subject"

In the context of this book, we are more focused on developing you as a **Leadership Coach,** which would then give us a more refined definition of:

"Someone who consciously empowers professionals (leaders or team members) through use of coaching principles, to develop their individual competencies"

h. **Coachee** – a coachee is the person receiving the coaching. In the context of Leadership Coaching, many times, the coachee will be your direct report. There are other situations, however, where you may coach other people in the organization, such as a peer, someone in another department, or even friends and family. Generally, in this context, you are not paid for your coaching services. You may receive some kind of gift as appreciation for your efforts, which is totally OK. In instances where there is a financial transaction, the coachee can also be referred to as a client.

i. **Sponsors** – Also known as Stakeholders. They are a third party who might be involved in arranging the coaching conversation between a coach and coachee. This is most common in paid coaching services, where an external coach is invited into the organization, to coach an employee. Typically, someone in HR or the direct supervisor will arrange such a meeting. In the context of INSTANT IMPACT Leadership Coaching, where the coaching conversations are shorter, a stakeholder or sponsor is not usually involved. The exception might be that your peer, in another department, is having challenges with a specific subordinate. They may ask you to 'have a chat' with them, to help address the challenge. That chat is a coaching conversation, and as such, should remain confidential between you and the coachee.

This covers most of the 'new' coaching terminology you may not have experienced before.

At its most fundamental, a coaching conversation is an intentional, structured conversation, that helps the other person (coachee) to 'think differently', to solve their own problems, and/or achieve their goals.

Chapter 3
What is Leadership Coaching and its Benefits

> *"Good leadership isn't about advancing yourself. It's about advancing your team."*
> — John C. Maxwell

Leadership Coaching is most easily defined as a Leader who utilizes coaching tools, techniques and strategies, to lead and empower his/her direct reports. This can be done individually, which may be referred to as 1-on-1 Coaching, or as Group Coaching, when working with a team or on a specific project. Additionally, Leadership Coaching can be conducted with other members within the organization, such as peer level, or other individuals at any level, within the organization.

As per the definitions outlined earlier, coaching is all about asking questions, instead of telling others what to do. This is a powerful way to develop and empower individuals and teams, as they are encouraged to think for themselves, get creative, and solve their own problems. We'll take a more detailed look at the benefits, a bit later.

It's important to clarify that you CANNOT coach all people, all of the time. As a Leader, you have many leadership tools and techniques at your disposal. Tools such as Direct Communication, Effective Feedback, Mentoring, and Facilitating, among many others.

Effective Leadership Coaching is designed to complement your current Leadership toolbox and should be used at the appropriate time, with the appropriate team member. To help clarify, let's look at the Leadership Development Matrix below:

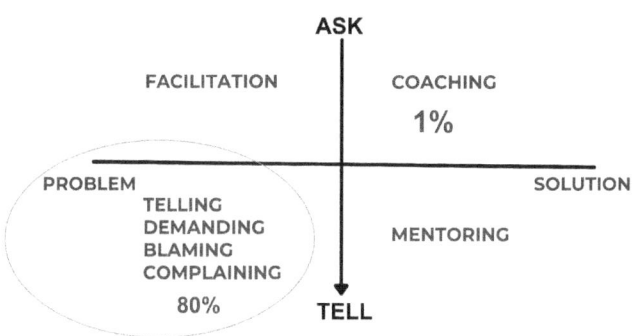

Consider this matrix as a guide to create a balanced Leadership style, whether for yourself, or for other leaders within your organization. Let's look at each quadrant.

The **bottom-left quadrant**, which focuses on the **Problem** and **Telling** people what to do, is where 80% of traditional Leaders spend most of their time. This is NOT empowering and often shows up us Demanding, Blaming and Complaining. Sometimes, of course it is necessary to TELL our teams what to do, but not 80% of the time. If we continually tell our teams what to do, we are not helping them to solve their own problems, which results in slower growth for the entire team. We also limit the entire team to our OWN level of thinking.

The **top-left quadrant** is typically the domain of Brainstorming, Problem Solving and Group Coaching, which initially focuses on a **Problem**, by **Asking** questions, to support the team to get to the root cause. Normally, these conversations start by focusing on the problem, and as you ask more questions, you get clearer on the root cause or the real underlying issue. We call this quadrant **Facilitation**. Once the core problem/challenge is identified, you begin to facilitate the session, by asking different questions that shift the focus toward a solution. As the Facilitator, you may 'know' the answer yourself, but by asking questions, you empower teams to think differently, get creative, and solve the problem themselves. Begin by asking questions to get really clear on the problem or challenge, then shift the direction of questions, by focusing on possible solutions.

The **bottom-right quadrant** is the domain of Mentoring. As we covered in the definitions, a mentor is typically 'really good' at a few specific things, so you will want to be **Telling** your Mentee (or team members) some possible tips, tricks or strategies that are focused on a **Solution**. Typically, as a great leader, chances are you're more skilled at general operations, problem-solving, dealing with urgent situations, etc. During instances where you might have time constraints, a longer Coaching Conversation may not be the best tool to use. As Mentoring involves a degree of Telling the lesser experienced person (Mentee) what to do, while focusing on the Solution, it can be a good way to arrive at solutions more quickly. Generally, the Mentor has 'done their push-ups', meaning that they have learned the hard way, and/or developed strategies, techniques, and processes to get results quickly. When these strategies are shared with the Mentee, you're giving them a recipe for success, which results in better results achieved more quickly.

The **top-right quadrant** is the domain of Coaching. Here, the Leader utilizes the key principles of Coaching, which is **Asking** questions, and focusing on **Solutions**. Surprisingly, most traditional Leaders only spend 1% of their Leadership time in this quadrant. That leaves massive room for improvement, empowerment, and supporting teams to solve their own challenges. By following the strategies outlined in this book, we suggest you start with your teams

10-twenty% of the time. Obviously, the time spent coaching will vary greatly, depending on the industry, team size, your additional roles and responsibilities, etc. Most importantly, you'll be able to conduct coaching conversations in twenty minutes or less, as you follow the guidelines. This will overcome the biggest obstacle to coaching… ' we don't have time to coach'. With practice, we encourage to coach your team twenty-30% of the time.

As a well-rounded Leader, you will want to develop all areas of your Leadership matrix. And as you grow to be the Leader of Leaders, you'll also want to support the Leaders under you, to have a well-balanced Leadership Development Matrix. A good guideline is as follows:

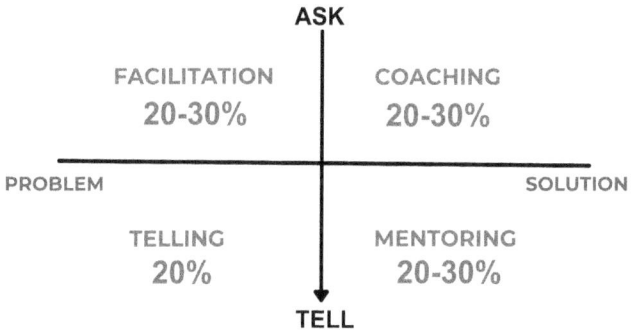

Different industries, your specific Leadership role, and the size of your team will affect how much time you spend in each quadrant. I've met senior Leaders who have built such a strong, dependable team, that they spend a whopping 80% of their time Coaching!!

One important distinction to consider, as you develop a more balanced Leadership Development matrix, is that you will be adjusting your overall Leadership and Communication style. You will move away from mostly telling, to a combination of asking, coaching and mentoring, with a small sprinkling of telling. That is a huge transition for your team. This means you will need to transition 'gently', from telling to asking, as your team has a certain perception of you. For example, let's assume you are one of those traditional leaders, who spend 80% of the time telling your teams what to do. You finish this book, research some more about coaching, and you get all fired up, declaring to yourself "I'm going to be an outstanding Leadership Coach", and you swing to the top right quadrant, and try to ASK questions 80% of the time. It's too much of a change, too quickly, for your team to embrace. Your team will be 'shocked', and they won't know how to respond to this dramatic change. They'll say things like:

> "I don't know boss, just tell me what to do."
> "You've always told us what to do."
> "Why are you asking so many questions"
> "Please just tell me"
> "Who are you, and what have you done with my boss?"
> No comments, just blank stares

This is why we recommend a gentle transition from that 80% telling, to just 10-20% of Coaching, in the beginning, to help the team transition to your new style of communication and leadership. This will help reduce any possible resistance from your team and will help you to fully integrate your new leadership style. In addition, as you also increase your percentages of Mentoring and Facilitation, you will be a well-rounded, empowering Leader.

Awareness and Action: for a few days, take note of your CURRENT Leadership style. Observe how much time you are spending in each quadrant. Keep a little diary or journal with you, and at the top of each hour, just make a few notes on what you were DOING.

Simple and Powerful Questions

The very process of asking questions to your teams, instead of telling them, helps them to think DIFFERENTLY. According to neuroscience, 90% of our thoughts, are the same as the day before. What this means is that if we continue to think those same thoughts, we will continue to make the same decisions, which then leads to the same behaviours and actions, which makes it really difficult to solve old, existing, and new challenges. Maintaining those same thoughts, behaviours, and actions, will make it very difficult to come up with new, innovative, or creative solutions. By asking your subordinates questions, you are helping them to think differently. You are asking them questions that they have not asked themselves. Those new questions, fire off new sets of neural networks in their brain, which leads to new thoughts, new ideas, new decisions, new actions, and ultimately, new solutions. By doing this, you help them to expand their thinking capacity and creativity, to solve even more problems and challenges, as they continue to grow. You've helped them develop a growth mindset, and you've helped them to solve their own problems. You've also helped them create the habit of solution focus, which empowers and elevates the entire team.

To help you with the transition from Telling to Asking, here is a framework to help you move from our typical tendency of Telling and Pushing, to Asking and Pulling:

Shifting Coaching focus from Telling to Asking

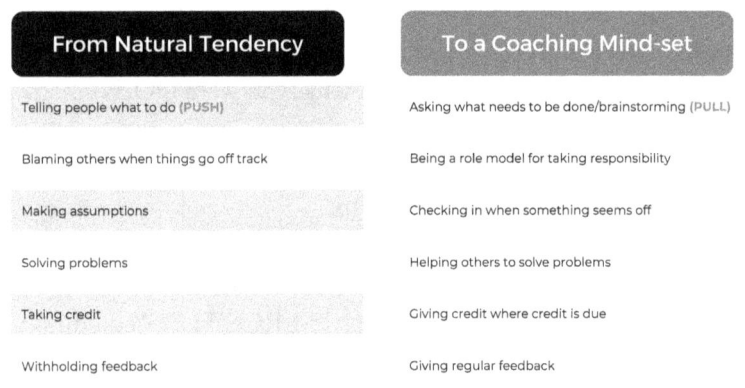

From Natural Tendency	To a Coaching Mind-set
Telling people what to do (PUSH)	Asking what needs to be done/brainstorming (PULL)
Blaming others when things go off track	Being a role model for taking responsibility
Making assumptions	Checking in when something seems off
Solving problems	Helping others to solve problems
Taking credit	Giving credit where credit is due
Withholding feedback	Giving regular feedback

In addition to the above framework, here are some very **simple and powerful questions**, that you can begin asking your teams, immediately, to help them think for themselves, and to support your gentle transition from telling to asking:

> What is on your mind?
> What do you think?
> What is one possibility?
> What could be one option?
> What could be another option?
> What else?
> I know you don't know, but if you did know?
> What would your role model recommend?
> What if it were easy?

What is missing?
What would I recommend you do?
What's the very next physical action?
What direct conversation can you have, to move this situation forward?
What if anything were possible?

This process alone, of simply asking powerful questions, will make a huge difference in the empowerment, creativity, and accountability of your team. You will see the instant impact!

My first real experience, as a subordinate, of my boss asking some of these powerful questions above, was many years ago, when I was working as a Front Office Manager in a resort on the tropical island of Koh Samui, Thailand. I had the pleasure of working with an amazing General Manager, who we will call Mr. John. Basically, I was his No.2 in the operation of the hotel, and we'd been working together for around 1 year. He had decided that the staff canteen, where all the staff have their meals, needed rebuilding because the resort was growing, along with the number of staff. In a resort, you typically have the main restaurant and kitchen, which is for guests to enjoy, and then at the back-of-house, you have the staff canteen, where their meals are prepared and eaten. Most Leaders would have had some plans drawn up, and then issued them directly to the engineer, and say 'build this'. Clearly, this is telling people what to do. Mr. John utilized a different strategy. He gathered all the Heads of Department (HOD) together, such as Head Chef, House Keeping, Engineer, Accounting, Front office manager (me), and a few others. He started by sharing the purpose of our meeting:

> "Today, I would like us to discuss the plan for the new staff canteen, and I would really appreciate everyone's input and ideas"

Then, very patiently, he asked each of us one by one:

"What do you think we should do?"

As each person shared, he wrote down their responses, acknowledged and encouraged them, and thanked them for their contribution. He then proceeded to the next person, repeating this process, carefully and deliberately with the 8 Leaders in attendance.

Now on this particular day, I had a wedding to organize on the beach, with fifty guests. I was getting a bit impatient, as we were now fifteen minutes into this conversation, and to me, it seemed 'easy' what we should do, to rebuild the staff canteen. In my naïve frustration, I blurted out:

"Mr. John, it's easy, we just knock that down, push that back, build a roof, and done. OK?! Can I go now", and off I dashed back down to the beach, to be 'busy' again.

About ten minutes later, Mr. John called me and said:

"Luke, can you come up to my office please?"

Not appreciating the seeming waste of time, I stormed up to his office and moaned:

"What ?!"

He calmly responded...

"Luke, thank you for almost ruining that whole process"

"What do you mean, it's easy to know what and how we should do it, why don't you just tell us?!" I replied, with a clear tone of frustration.

"Luke" he gently replied "if I tell them what to do, they won't take ownership, it will take twice as long to complete, and I'll have to check-in multiple times per day" he continued "But if I ask them 'what do you think', they will take ownership of their ideas, they will probably come up with better ideas than I could have thought by myself, and they have greater accountability, so they'll probably complete the project in half the time, without me having to regularly follow up. Plus, they will be proud of themselves because THEY did it!!"

"Ohhhhhhh, I see" was my amazed and somewhat humbled response.

The penny dropped. I got it, and it rocked my world. How can something so simple as just asking questions, be such a powerful tool for greater efficiency and productivity? I could see how asking questions SAVED time. More on this later...

I immediately adopted this new style of Leadership, asking questions, within my own Leadership journey. Within four months, I landed a GM role in another hotel, doubling my salary, and inspiring me to discover the art and science behind these coaching questions and strategies.

Awareness and Action: Building on the awareness you created from the Leadership Development Matrix, begin to gently shift your Communication and Leadership style to more asking and less telling. Simply change your 'language' by asking some of the simple and powerful questions outlined earlier, and watch the magic unfold. Try this for one full week.

Benefits of Coaching Your Teams

Now that you have a clear understanding of what Leadership Coaching IS, and how it is aligned with other Leadership modalities, it's time to drill down, to develop a clearer understanding of all the benefits of Leadership Coaching. In summary, the key benefits you can expect are:

a. Empower others, by getting them to think differently, and solve their own problems
b. Coaching as a Return on Investment (ROI) of time
c. Coaching develops greater Loyalty and less turn-over
d. Coaching creates greater inspiration and motivation in individuals and teams
e. Coaching helps develop greater resilience and higher EQ
f. Coaching enhances Succession Planning and delegation
g. Coaching develops your skills as a Leader

Let's take a look at these benefits of Coaching in more detail:

Empower others, by getting them to think differently, and solve their own problems

As we outlined earlier, the same level of thinking cannot solve problems at the same level of thinking that created them. Thinking is an internal conversation that someone has with themselves, asking questions and coming up with answers. During coaching conversations, we ask our teams different questions, to help them think differently, and therefore come up with different answers, solutions, and ways forward. With repetition of these quality questions, your subordinate will begin to ask themselves those same quality questions, which will help them come up with quality answers and solutions, all by themselves. In doing so, you empower them to the next level of success.

Coaching is a Return on Investment (ROI) of time

If you give me $1000 and I give you back $5000, that is a great Return on Investment (ROI). This same principle can be applied with TIME as you begin coaching your teams. We think that telling our teams what to do is a more efficient use of time, as it takes just a few minutes to give an order or instructions. The challenge with that modality is that we are not helping our teams to think for themselves and therefore, they aren't growing. We assume that asking questions and having a coaching conversation takes a long time, or that we "don't have time for this".

We need to create a new paradigm and realize that YES, it does take a little extra time to ask questions, and, that extra time, is an investment of time. In the beginning, you will invest approximately one to two hours per month, per subordinate, in coaching conversations and asking questions. Within one to three months, you will start to 'cash in' on that investment, as you will have empowered your teams to think for themselves and solve their own problems. Instead of running back to you every hour or two with a new problem, they will be more proactive, more creative, and take greater ownership of their own situations. This will save you hours, and eventually days, of your time. This means that those one to two coaching hours invested per month will save you two, five, or seven days, over the course of one year, for each one of your subordinates!!

Remember the story of Mr. John, and how he applied asking questions in a group coaching context? That new staff canteen was seemingly built in record time, with less drama than I'd ever experienced with any kind of hotel project or construction. I calculated that Mr. John, through his approach of asking 'what do you think' saved 4 weeks off the overall project completion, and hours of his own time, with less need for follow-up. A huge return on his investment of time, with that thirty-minute meeting!!

Coaching for Succession Planning

Old school leadership generally meant that I didn't want to share HOW I did my job as a Leader, with anyone else, for fear that they would steal my job. Leaders would deliberately keep a big gap between their 'level' of skills and capabilities, to those under their command. The problem with that is it stunts the entire team's skills and capabilities to your own level. And obviously, you are not growing as a Leader, either. Consider these two scenarios:

> Scenario#1
> Leader: 'Hey boss, I'd like to take a two-week vacation to travel abroad'
> Boss: 'Well. I'd love to give you that time off, but who will take care of your department while you're gone? In fact, every time you take leave, your

department becomes a mess. Sorry, the maximum I can give you is five days'

Scenario#2
Leader: 'Hey boss, I'd like to put my hand up for that promotion to that new role as division head'
Boss: 'Well, I'd love to give you that opportunity to grow, but who will oversee your department if you grow to the next level? No one is up to the task. Sorry, it can't be done"

The above are the consequences of NOT pro-actively planning for your own succession!

In reality, a good leader will want to develop their team to ensure succession planning, team competence and strength within the organisation or group.

As you coach and mentor your team, and help them develop their skills, capabilities, and responsibilities, they grow. You can begin to close the gap between you and them. Through this process, you also grow, and so the only way is UP. The best way to facilitate this process is to start thinking about a succession plan. In other words, which person (or people) within your department, can you begin to groom and develop, so that they can fulfill your role? You MUST close that gap between your skill level and their skill level. As you plan your successor, the next immediate action you must take is effective delegation, and coaching is a great way to support the delegation process. Remember, delegation is not dumping. Delegating will be a combination of Coaching, Mentoring, and perhaps even some training, to help upskill your subordinate to the next level. If your goal is to accelerate your leadership journey, get good at delegation and succession planning, and your growth is assured. If you consciously develop your teams and close the gap, those above conversations with your boss become very different, as follows:

> Scenario#1
> Leader: 'Hey boss, I'd like to take a two-week vacation to travel abroad'
> Boss: 'Absolutely. You've done such a great job empowering your teams that I feel very confident your team will take care of things while you are away. Enjoy !!'
>
> Scenario#2
> Leader: "Hey boss, I'd like to put my hand up for that promotion to that new role as division head"
> Boss: "I'm pleased to hear that. I've seen the effort you've put into developing your succession plan, along with the coaching and mentoring you've been facilitating with your team. Let's discuss the next steps..."

Coaching for Greater Loyalty

Studies have shown that a **lack of opportunity for Growth** is one of the biggest reasons why people leave organizations. As a Leader, you must show interest and importance to continually develop your teams. Coaching, as a Leader, is a great way to show that you care for your team's growth and development. This in turn creates massive loyalty and less turnover. As you coach your teams to step out of their comfort zones, as you show belief that they can succeed with that 'difficult' project or task, and as you coach them to develop personally and professionally, it distills within them greater self-confidence. 'Wow, if the boss believes I can do it, maybe I CAN do it !!'

Coach your teams at every opportunity. Show them that their growth is important to you, and they will reward you with unshakeable loyalty.

Awareness and Action: Begin to notice the immediate benefits both you and your team receive from Leadership Coaching. For best results, focus on one of the benefits for one week, and journal your awareness and results. For the next week, focus on one of the other benefits. After just two months, these new benefits will form an integral part of your Leadership, and your results as a team.

Chapter 4
Overcoming the three biggest obstacles to resistance

"You will never find time for anything. If you want time, you must make it."

— Charles Buxton

Overcoming the three biggest obstacles to resistance

As we touched on earlier, we cannot coach all of the people, all of the time. There are a few reasons for this, namely:

1. Inflated Ego – in either the Coach or Coachee
2. Lack of Rapport – Trust and Connection
3. Lack of Time – as perceived by either the Coachee and/or the Coach

As we become aware of this resistance, we can best plan for it, prevent it and overcome it. The more you can prevent the resistance, the more INSTANT the IMPACT will be with your coachee. Let's explore each in more detail, to ensure your coaching conversations are most effective.

1. **Inflated Ego**

A strong ego in your coachee can make the coaching process very difficult. A strong ego often comes across as 'I know everything', or 'I'm not the problem, it's my twenty subordinates that are the problem'. With that kind of attitude, it's hard to support them to grow and improve, which is why it's at the top of the list.

In someone with a strong ego, who do they think is the most important person in the room (or organization)? Correct, Themselves!! A strong ego is declaring to the world that 'I know everything, I don't need to improve, I have nothing to learn'. And when dealing with that type of behavior inside a coaching conversation, it becomes near impossible to achieve any progress.

There can be a few reasons WHY people display this inflated ego, and while it's technically not within the scope of this book, I do want to touch on the root cause of this kind of behavior, so that you have greater awareness, along with the possibility to support their growth.

Generally, this type of person is trying to fulfill their ***need for significance*** or importance. It often (not always) stems from childhood and adolescence challenges, where they did not feel appreciated, loved, or supported. They may even seek adult relationships, where this type of 'drama' is continued, which makes their only source of significance and importance the workplace. As you can imagine, the role of a 'boss' is a great opportunity for this type of individual to fulfill this basic human need. Just like we have the need for Certainty in our Life (food, shelter, water, etc.), this basic human need for significance is a very unconscious driver of our behaviors. Discover more about these fundamental human needs with Tony Robbins explanation of the Six Human Needs.

There can be 'healthy' or productive ways to fulfill this need, and there can be unproductive or harmful ways to fulfill this need.

Individuals with the inflated ego, are trying to find and fulfill their significance in many counter-productive ways, such as:

- being demanding
- belittling others
- yelling and anger
- being super 'busy'
- being better-than
- having the last word
- Ridiculing, shaming and complaining

The reason I share this with you is not to become judgmental of this type of behavior, but to develop empathy for individuals that display these characteristics. Showing empathy can open doors for a much deeper and more powerful coaching conversation.

Another term I've heard, that describes this kind of ego relating to the above, is the **Protective Personality**. Because the individual has been 'hurt' in the past, they build up a barrier and defence mechanism, that prevents others from getting too close.

One good tactic when working with someone with a strong ego is to make it all about them. Because we know that they crave the need for Significance, we need to help them feel significant, which helps them feel safe and more open. They already believe that the universe should revolve around them, so 'stroke' their ego a little, to help build rapport. For example:

- "What do YOU want to achieve…"
- "What is YOUR outcome…"
- "I know the problem is 'over there', but what do YOU want to focus on…"

- "What is within YOUR control"
- "As you are the expert in this area, please share YOUR ideas/concerns…"

With awareness and application of the above, you should have success in opening up a coaching conversation. As with all coaching development, practice is key, so just keep doing your best in every coaching conversation you have. Failing the use of the above, you would simply need to use a more direct form of communication (instead of coaching), such as direct feedback, involving Human Resources, or possibly even disciplinary action

Here are a few more phrases and examples that you could practice, with someone displaying egotistical behavior.

> Coach: "I'm not really sure why HR sent you to see me, I don't see any problem. Regardless of what they think, can you tell me what YOU would like to explore, or what goals YOU would like to achieve?"

> Coach: "I'm not here to 'fix' you, clearly, you're not broken. I'm simply here as a support, to help you achieve the next level of success. Can you tell me what the next level looks like to YOU?"

> Coach: "It doesn't matter what 'they' want, you tell me what YOU want"

> Coach: "I know you're busy, and this could be a waste of both our time. So please tell me, what would make this coaching process great for YOU?"

> Coach: "Listen, we are stuck together whether we like it or not. YOU tell me, HOW we can make this time together useful?"
>
> Coach: (risky option) "OK look, that is a waste of both our times. It's probably best I inform the sponsor, and we end this right now…"
>
> The key point here is…find out what THEY (the coachee) want. What is their outcome, their motivation, and their leverage point? Find that, and utilize it for best results…

The awareness of the above is not to judge or criticize someone, but to develop greater empathy, and to help the coachee re-discover their greatness.

Whoever you coach, there is one principle that I strongly recommend you incorporate into your coaching mindset:

As a great Coach, we must believe the Coachee is **Whole, Creative and Resourceful.**

As with the strong ego in our Coachee, we also need to be mindful of the strong ego in ourselves!!

Generally speaking, the BEST coaches are Curious, Humble and embody a Growth Mindset. A great coach knows that they don't know everything and that there are many things that they don't know that they don't know. A great coach is a continuous learner, continually seeking a deeper understanding of human behavior, leadership strategies, and better ways to communicate and motivate. The trap for new coaches is that after a few quick 'wins' and successes, the ego can creep in. That feeling of 'better-than'. Be mindful that your success doesn't go to your head, but instead goes to your heart. If you become too arrogant, egotistical, or better-than, it does not create a safe space for your Coachee to open up, and your coaching conversation will be very shallow and surface-level, and therefore, not very effective. Always be humble and curious, and you will be assured of an amazing coaching conversation and continual growth and fulfillment.

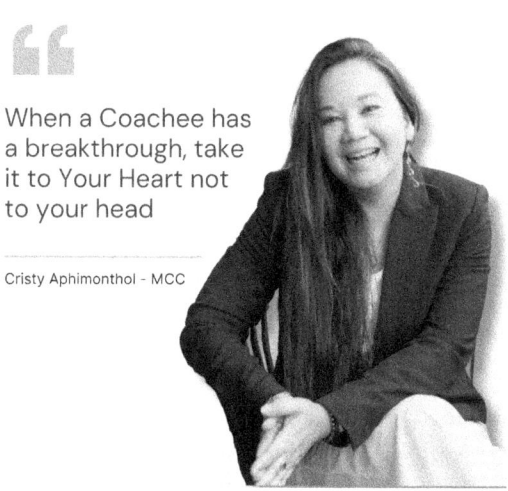

> When a Coachee has a breakthrough, take it to Your Heart not to your head
>
> Cristy Aphimonthol - MCC

2. Lack of Rapport – Trust and Connection

Rapport is that FEELING of Trust and Connection with another human. You have it with your close friends, your partner, and your family (most of the time). Think of those deep and personal conversations you've had with your best friend. You KNEW they would keep that conversation private, you felt safe to fully open up, to be vulnerable, to share. That same feeling is the feeling that you need to create with your Coachee. Without it, the coaching conversation will simply be a chit-chat and will stay at the surface level.

During your coaching journey, you will experience many types of Coachee, with varying problems, challenges, and goals. Some of them will be like an open book. They will dive deep into the details very quickly and openly share their darkest secrets. For most Coachee though, they take a little time to 'warm up' and therefore, to feel safe, and ultimately open up.

Your job here as a Coach, whether it's Leadership Coaching with your teams, or with paying clients, is your ability to quickly build trust. The more trust you can build, the more open your coachee will be. The more open they are, the deeper they will dive into the likely root cause of the situation, and powerful actions that will help them move forward.

Remember a time in the past, when you worked with a colleague or boss that you simply didn't trust or like? Chances are, you minimized your communication and interaction with them, as much as you could. Your coachee will be the same if they don't trust you.

Rapport, that ability to build trust and respect, is a soft skill that can be developed. Some are naturally good at it, while some take a little more time. However good you are at currently building rapport, you need to go deeper, much deeper, to provide the safest possible space for your coachee to explore the unknown and achieve instant impact.

A more modern concept that is fully aligned with Rapport is called Psychological Safety, which by definition states:

> "A belief that one will not be humiliated or punished for speaking up with ideas, questions, concerns or mistakes" – Amy Edmondson

You must be able to create a safe environment that encourages your coachee to speak up, without fear of judgment, humiliation, or punishment.

Here are 5 behaviors that we encourage you to embody, as both a Coach and Leader, to encourage more open communication and dialogue, with your teams:

1. **Awareness** – If you truly want to connect to the person you're communicating with, do your best to be totally present. Remove any distractions, center yourself, and non-judgmentally observe your coachee. How's their communication style? Are they distracted? Are they open? Are they 'big picture' or detailed? Are they calm or agitated? Are they stressed, worried, or concerned, or are they happy, light and enthusiastic? No judgments here, just awareness. If you are not present, thinking about all the other things you need to do today, or the grocery list you need to pick up at 7-11 on the way home, then you are not aware and have less opportunity to truly connect with, and positively impact your coachee.
2. **Listen** – Generally, we are so busy talking 'at' people all the time. Do this, do that, do the other, that we rarely stop and *really listen* to the individuals within our teams. We need to talk *with our teams*, not 'at' them. The easiest way to become a better listener is to simply ask more questions, which is coaching 101. If you intend to ask more questions, please make sure you also intend to listen, as you may discover something that you don't know that you don't know. People just want to be heard, so allowing a safe space for people to simply vent and share their frustrations is like a deposit in their emotional bank account. Whatever amount of listening you're doing right now… double it!
3. **Empathy** – step into your client's shoes and imagine feeling how they might feel. This is easy if you have gone through a similar situation that they are presenting to you, and not so easy if you've not experienced it before. Either way, try and appreciate and respect what they might be going through.

What may seem like an 'easy' fix to you (because of your Life's experience) may be deeply troubling and traumatic for the coachee,

4. **Non-Judgmental** – do you like that feeling of being judged or ridiculed? No, of course not. So don't do it. It really is that simple. Often, as a Coach, you need to have a greater belief and faith in your coachee, than they have in themselves. We need to believe that they can overcome the challenge and achieve their goal. We are often our biggest critics, and that self-judgment holds many of us back, even with good intentions and the loftiest of goals. As a Coach, you need to be the opposite. You are the cheerleader, the raving fan, and the number one supporter of your coachee. That continued encouragement and support will inspire them to take more 'risks', to get outside of their comfort zone more often, and take the actions necessary to achieve their success.

5. **Pace and Lead** – As we touched on before, some coachees are an open book, some are closed off and guarded, and others are somewhere in between. Your role is to connect with the client (build rapport) and then move the conversation forward at their pace and speed. If you push some people too quickly, they will shut down. If you move too slowly with others, they'll get bored, and you'll lose their respect. Pacing and Leading is like a dance, and each coaching conversation that you have is a dance in the moment. Even the same client may have a different speed from week to week, conversation to conversation. We don't know what kind of week they've had, what happened this morning, or even what happened just before your coaching conversation. Starting with your awareness, you will adjust your pace and speed to help the client feel safe and comfortable, stretching them ever so slightly, but not breaking.

"Resistance in a Client is lack of Rapport"

Resistance in your Coachee can show up in many ways. Some common examples:

- not opening up/being closed
- turning up late or not at all
- not completing tasking/actions
- easily distracted
- one word/very short responses

In any of these instances, the root cause of their resistance is a lack of rapport, and the solution is an easy one … Build more Rapport! Embody those five behaviors mentioned above, and you will be assured of deeper, more meaningful conversations. A few more tips to build rapport:

1. Find something in common/mutual interest
2. Pay a genuine compliment
3. Match their communication style – body language, tone of voice, words used
4. Be mindful of your own communication style
5. Show genuine appreciation

Awareness and Action: for a few days, really focus on developing Rapport with ALL your Team, Colleagues, and Co-Workers. Advance this skill even more by practicing with total strangers, such as waiters, convenience store cashiers, or any other person you interact with in your daily endeavours. Build this muscle now, and keep practicing, for better Leadership and Coaching results.

3. **Lack of Time - We don't have time to Coach or be Coached**
This is one of the biggest resistances you'll have, especially inside a company as you implement your Leadership Coaching practices.

Even with all of today's modern technology, apps and software, it seems we have even LESS time available than we did twenty years ago.

When it comes to 'not having enough time', this generally shows up in two ways:

1. Yourself not having enough time
2. The Coachee not having enough time

Let's start with the time management that you CAN control – Yourself!!

The best way to overcome this objection for yourself is by being aware that Coaching is a 'Return on Investment (ROI) of YOUR Time'. What this means is that for every hour you invest in coaching your teams, your ROI will be anywhere from two to five hours in the short term, two to three days in the medium term, and weeks and months in the longer term.

For example, let's say that over the course of one month, you Coach Fred for a total of two hours. It could be a couple of fifteen-minute conversations, a few twenty-minute conversations, and maybe a longer thirty-minute conversation. Typically, one of the most organic ways you can begin to coach your teams is when they come running to you with a problem.

Practicing your newly found coaching skills, you know not to TELL Fred how to fix his problem. Instead, you will ask some of those simple and powerful coaching questions we identified earlier, to help Fred come up with three options and possibilities, and then supporting him to choose the best action:

- What do you think you could do

- What could be another option
- What is one more
- What would I recommend you do
- Which one of those will help you achieve your outcome

A few days later, Fred comes back with another problem, and you repeat the same process. Patiently asking those questions, and helping Fred solve his own problem.

Then, something magic happens. On the third or fourth 'problem', Fred says to himself "You know what…I think I can solve this problem myself". And he does!!

At that moment, you begin to 'cash in' on your investment of time. You've invested two hours over one month with Fred. You've helped him articulate his problems and challenges more clearly, you've supported him to think strategically by considering various options and alternatives, and you've encouraged him to make the best decisions. You've helped him grow and solve more of his own problems.

So now, he doesn't need to run back to you every few hours with his next problem. He is more proactive, more resourceful, and is more accountable….he can simply get on with things. And this is where you save YOUR time, because of fewer interruptions, less putting out 'fires', and less micro-managing.

You will start to see your return on your investment within two to three short months.

A nice little story or metaphor may be useful, to help explain this most important benefit of Coaching. Remember my little story about Mr. John and the staff canteen at the resort? This can be useful to help get buy-in from upper management.

From the coachees perspective, a few things need to happen for them to be OK with the time they need to invest in the coaching process. We'll list them down in point form for simplicity:

1. Share with them all the benefits of Coaching
2. Explain the ROI concept of Coaching
3. Agree to consistent, short powerful sessions, of around twenty minutes
4. Schedule the sessions into a calendar. What gets scheduled, gets done
5. Potentially, you may need to link a 'painful' consequence to missed or canceled sessions, such as informing the sponsors or buying a coffee (let the coachee decide the consequence)

Overall, both the sponsor and the coachee need to be made aware that Coaching is an **ROI of time**. Another great example you can share, for the coachee or sponsor would be...

As a Leader, you constantly have your team running up to you..."Boss, Boss, there is a problem, there is a problem". Traditional leadership would simply TELL your staff how to fix the problem, as we believe that's the quickest way. The challenge with that is that we are not empowering our teams to solve their own problems. In addition, when we have many of our team running up to us, it adds up to a LOT of wasted time.

Instead, we need to create the new habit of asking them "What do you think you should do" when they come running to you with their 'problem'. Initially, they'll respond with "I don't know" and this is where you need to be patient, and gently ask again "Come on, I know you have a recommendation". With time, practice and patience, you will elicit solutions from them. After you practice this new habit for a month or so, one day, your employee won't be running back to you. He'll say to himself

"If I go running to the boss, he's just going to ask me 'what do you think you should do'. You know what, I can solve this myself."

So again, through asking these Coaching questions, while it is an investment of time initially, as you empower your teams, you will save yourself hours and days of your time, while they grow at the same time. Win-Win!!

A very organic way to practice your coaching and empower others is when they come to you with problems. It happens more than you think. When you have that opportunity to invest ten to twenty minutes in that coaching conversation, then do it.

Another very natural way to practice your coaching skills is during any form of brainstorming. Whether it's trying to get to the root cause of a problem, developing an action plan, working on KPI development, or a Professional Development Plan (PDP), when you resist the urge to tell everyone how to do it, you simply ask more questions. Even though you might know the problem (if you're trying to find the root cause or main source of the problem) or if you're working on the solution, you do not tell your team the answers. Guide them by asking powerful questions. Soon enough, they'll be able to facilitate those sessions themselves, saving you hours and hours of your time.

Awareness and Action: For the first month or two of your coaching practice, whether it's asking these simple powerful questions outlined previously, or using the full POW Coaching Model, keep a record of the actual time spent coaching. Then, also monitor how much time you have saved, through the pro-activeness of your team. It might be a little tricky to assess and do your best to measure it.

Chapter 5
Correct SMART Goal Setting - We've been doing it wrong

"You get what you Focus on, so Focus on what you want"
– Steve Mehr

Goal
"The object of a person's ambition or effort: an aim or desired result."

A goal is an outcome, a destination, the desired result.

Before we get into the details, let's have some fun. On the following two blank pages, I'd like to write down ANY and ALL the goals you'd like to achieve in the next thirty years. Write the big ones, the small ones, the crazy ones, the outrageous ones. The impossible ones, the forbidden ones. Whatever they are for you, write them down. Don't hold back, go WILD, and fill both pages. This is your chance to shine. Don't limit yourself. Imagine if ANYTHING were possible. Imagine achieving them was easy. Don't start thinking about HOW to achieve them, just focus on what you want, what you desire, what you need, and what you deserve. These are YOUR goals. They can be any area of your Life. Work, Business, Health, Relationships, Spirituality, EQ, Personal Development, Education, places to visit. Whatever it is for you, write them ALL down. Are you ready?? Go…

Great!! Well done. How does that feel? If you haven't done the exercise yet, please do so before moving forward. When your Coachee shares their goals with you, they will somehow be like some of the goals you just wrote above.

By the way, can you come back to these pages and add more goals as you think of them? Of course you can!! These are YOUR goals; this is YOUR future.

So, you have two pages of goals you want to achieve. Great!! Now it's time to get a little clearer and decide 'by when' you'd like to achieve those goals. Quickly review all those goals you just wrote down, and beside each one, simply write a number next to it, which represents how many years you think it will take you, to achieve that goal. If it's a five-year goal, just write the number 5 next to it, or 5 with a circle around it. If it's a longer-term goal, write a 10 next to it. For a shorter-term goal, write a 2 next to it. If it is a one-year goal, simply write a 1 next to that goal. If it will take less than one year to achieve, such as within three months, still write a 1 next to it. OK, clear? Go ahead, and write down how many years it will take you, to achieve each goal…

All done? Great. The next step is to take ALL the goals with a 1 written next to them, which means you wish to achieve that goal within one year or less and write them down freshly on this next blank page. Chances are, you have around five to ten goals that you wish to achieve in one year or less. Go ahead, and write those down freshly now…

Fantastic!! This is a little pre-work that you've just completed, as we dig deeper into correct SMART goal setting. How does it feel to have completed the above exercise? Excited? Motivated? Inspiring? Or maybe you feel overwhelmed? Heavy? Thinking it's impossible? Whatever your thoughts and feelings, just notice them. It's the very first step to creating the Life you want.

This exercise you just completed above is also a great exercise that you can facilitate with groups, to help 'get the juices' flowing, in terms of creativity, getting outside of their heads, and really opening up to new possibilities. Remember, we are not yet focusing on HOW to achieve these goals yet. We still need to correctly structure them as a SMART Goal, so let's keep going…

Without a clear destination, how can we get to where we want to go? The most basic, fundamental action we can take when wanting to grow to the next level of success, whether personal, professional or as a team, is to have a clear goal. A clear destination that we can work towards.

Think about your GPS or Google maps…whenever I am driving somewhere I am not familiar with, I ALWAYS open up Google maps on my phone, and type in the final destination. The EXACT destination. Not a vague destination, not an approximate destination, the EXACT destination. if you don't correctly enter the final destination, you'll get lost, waste time, waste money, waste resources, and get very frustrated. You'll simply end up somewhere else, and NOT arrive at your final destination.

That's why goals are like the final destination in your google maps. If it's not clear, you'll get lost, and not achieve your goal. It's extremely important in any Coaching Conversation, to create absolute clarity and certainty on the final destination. This helps create the instant impact you're looking for.

There have been dozens of books written on Goal setting, and while we won't go into massive detail here, it is important to spend some time on clearly defining HOW to correctly structure a SMART Goal.

Before we do that, I'd like to expand on the neuroscience and psychology of the human brain, so that we can utilize its full power for the goal-setting process. Essentially, our brain is divided into two parts…our Conscious brain, and our subconscious brain. Not to be confused with the left brain and right brain, which may be defined as the logical side and the creative side.

The conscious mind is defined as what we are aware of (conscious of) in this moment of time.

Therefore, the subconscious mind must be everything that we are NOT consciously aware of. The things within our knowledge and experience, and the things that we don't know that we don't know. Said another way, it's the things that we are not aware of, at this moment.

You can think of your conscious mind as a flashlight. Whatever you focus on, has the attention of your conscious mind. For example, can you hear or feel your heart beating? Hopefully, you answered yes. Was it always beating? Of course it was, but you were unaware of it, until it was mentioned. You moved your focus to become conscious of your heart beating. Another example…can you feel your toes? I bet you can now!! So again, your focus shifted, for that moment, to your toes, as you wiggled them.

Scientific studies have shown that we are only conscious 5% of the day. That means that 95% of the day, we are unconscious, running on our subconscious programming. In other words, we are running on a set of programs and habits, so we don't have to consciously 'think' about that stuff. Here are some great examples of what our subconscious mind handles:

- Breathing (without thinking)
- Heart beating
- Walking
- Eating
- Digestion
- Cleaning your teeth
- Getting dressed
- Any skill or sport you're good at – golf, tennis, running, etc.
- Driving (although it wasn't always easy, you practiced and practiced, and through repetition, you learned how to do it easily, it became a habit, a program)

The subconscious mind is also the realm of memories, just like a HUGE filing cabinet. Even though you cannot consciously remember everything all at once, all of your memories, from the day you were born, are stored in the subconscious mind. These memories can be accessed through questions, for example – can you remember your first successful sports event, such as winning a trophy, kicking a goal, or winning a race? Questions help direct the focus of the flashlight, the conscious mind, to search through that filing cabinet, to retrieve the memory.

Very importantly, the subconscious mind is also the realm of your emotions. Our emotions are bio-chemical releases in the body, that determine how we feel, moment to moment. Most of the time, it is automatic and unconscious, and many people do not exercise much conscious control over their emotions. Yet, neuroscience tells us that our moment-to-moment thoughts (conscious or unconscious) primarily determine our emotions, and how we feel.

Try this exercise – think of a really pleasant memory. A time when you felt totally happy. As you think of that time, notice what you saw, hear what you heard, and really really feel the feeling that you felt. Notice how great those feelings feel. Hold those thoughts and feelings for a few moments. How do you feel right now? Chances are you're even happier than before, which proves that our thoughts affect our feelings.

So, what does this have to do with SMART goals? Well, because emotions reside in the subconscious mind, which is 95% of your brain power, you want to link your positive emotions to your goals. The more positive emotion attached to your goal, the more motivated and proactive you will be towards achieving your goal. We'll dive a little deeper into emotions throughout the book.

Typically, when writing a goal down, is it a conscious process or a subconscious process?

The answer of course is conscious. Based on our learnings above, if that goal were to remain only in the conscious realm of thought, we are using just 5% of our total brain capacity. What about that additional 95% of our subconscious mind? How can we tap into it?

Said in a much simpler way:

The Conscious Mind is the Goal Setter, and the Subconscious Mind is the Goal Getter

What we must do is take that SMART goal, structure it correctly, and lock it into the subconscious mind. Create a habit and a program around that goal, so that your subconscious mind is always working on ways, on how to achieve that goal for you…even while you sleep!!

We need to take our SMART goal from sitting on the surface (5% conscious mind), and 'install' it into the 95% of the subconscious mind.

Let's explore a little bit more about how the subconscious mind functions, especially in the context of creating habits and programs.

Our subconscious mind is continually looking for patterns of behaviour and repetition. It's basically a pattern recognition machine. When the subconscious mind notices that you continually repeat a task or activity, the Subconscious mind says:

"Oh. This must be really important. The 'boss' keeps focusing on this task and keeps repeating it again and again. Here, let me create a program (habit) for that task and take care of that, so you can focus on other things."

Remember when you learned to drive a car? When you first learned to drive a car, it was difficult: stop, start, grind gears and whoever was teaching you was maybe a little bit scared. Slowly, with practice and repetition the subconscious mind says 'Ahhh, this is important. Let me take that task and make it automated. Let me 'write a program' for that thing that you're doing a lot. Let me make it a habit for you so that you can consciously focus on other things.'

This process is true for any habit that you have created. Good ones and bad ones. You see, the subconscious mind doesn't know the difference between good and bad or right and wrong. It only notices what you continually focus on and repeat.

What if we could take these same principles of habit creation, and utilize them to 'lock in' our SMART goal into the subconscious mind? Would that help us achieve our goals more easily and effortlessly?

We need to take the goal from that surface conscious level, and get it embedded into our subconscious mind, because then we are utilizing that extra 95% of our subconscious mind. And because the subconscious mind is the goal getter, we are automatically driven and motivated to get out there and achieve that goal, doing whatever it takes, because that's how the subconscious mind has been programmed.

It's like a magic genie that helps us achieve our goals. A correctly structured SMART goal would not just be conscious surface level, it will be embedded into the subconscious mind as well.

Before we go deeper into SMART Goal setting, let's first understand why most traditional SMART Goals DON'T Work. Quite simply:

1. They are NOT Simple
2. They are NOT Date Specific
3. They are NOT Focused on

They are NOT simple - Have you ever noticed that most corporate or organizational goals are loooooong and complicated? Sure, you and your big boss might understand them, but sadly, your team and your subconscious mind do NOT understand them. They are meaningless numbers and words. Here's a typical example:

> We want to achieve 3% growth on the previous quarter's profit margins by the end of the fiscal year

Huh?! There is so much vagueness and lack of clarity in that statement. Companies wonder why they struggle to achieve their goals and KPIs.

They are NOT date Specific – Interestingly, the T in traditional SMART goals means Timely or Timeframe. Yet, most goals I see when working with new corporate clients are worded as follows...

- we achieve xxx by end of the month
- we achieve xxx by end of the 3rd QTR
- we achieve xxx by the beginning of the year
- we achieve xxx by end of the fiscal year

Once again, you and the big boss may know what that means, but most of your staff do not, and your subconscious mind, that extra 95% of your brain, does not.

They are not focused on – most goals are created during some form of brainstorming, KPI development, or action planning. They're written up on some flip charts, which at the end of the day get rolled up, and stashed under HR's desk, only to be thrown out six months later. Zero focus goes towards those goals, and as a result, limited success.

As a quick review, let's clearly define the original or traditional model, where SMART is an acronym for:

S = Specific
M = Measurable
A = Achievable
R = Relevant
T = Timely

The new improved version for correct SMART Goal setting is:

S = Specific and Simple
M = Measurable and Meaningful
A = Achievable and Agreed

R = Relevant and Realistic
T = Timely and Towards outcome

The reasons why this new model is more effective are as follows:

- it overcomes those main reasons why traditional SMART goals don't work
- It integrates with the subconscious mind
- It's more accurate
- It works for individuals and teams

Let's expand on each for a clearer understanding…

Specific and Simple – you want your SMART goal to be structured in such a super specific way, and, as short and simple as possible. It should be so simple, that you could walk up to anyone on the street, show them your goal, and they would understand what you want to achieve. This is important, because your subconscious mind, that 95% of your brain power, is like a 4-year-old child. This means that when using language, you want to be clear, precise and simple as possible. Here are some examples of goals that are NOT specific enough:

- I want to be rich
- I wish I was healthy
- I don't want to be fat
- I don't want to get angry every time I see my boss's face
- Increase sales by 10%
- Increase revenue by 5% from last quarter

These are not specific enough because there is no way to specifically capture and analyse any data. They sound like most non-SMART goals, but they're not specific.

Measurable and Meaningful – By measurable we mean 'how will you know that you've achieved your goal'. I want 1,000,000 USD in the bank. Can you measure that? Yes, easily, with a bank statement. I want to be 80kg. Again, easily measured by stepping onto the scales. Whatever your goal, you must have a measurement so that you know you've achieved it.

What about a less tangible goal, such as 'I want to be happier' or 'I'd like to be more confident' …how do you measure that? One good way with this type of goal is to 'scale' the current situation and desired situation. Here is a typical goal-elicitation conversation with your coachee:

Coachee: I want to be happier
Coach: OK, good. on a scale of 1-10, how would you rate your happiness now?
Let the coachee answer: Ummmm, a 5 (or whatever 'score' they give)
Coach: OK, what would you like it to be instead?
Coachee: Ummm, an 8 (or whatever new score they give)
Coach: OK great!! And how will you know that you're an 8 out of 10?

Now, just let them answer in their own way. Your coachees will give various answers of HOW they measure their Happiness, Success, Confidence, or whatever it is that they are measuring:

Coachee: I'll know I'm an 8/10 when … (whatever they say)

Let them speak, let them vent, let them explore. This is not the time to impose your own measure of 'happiness', as it means so many different things to so many different people.

Meaningful, is also the M of the SMART goal, and it means that there is emotion involved. If something is meaningful, you feel a deep sense of connection, motivation and inspiration. Something that does not have any meaning for you, reduces the inspiration and the motivation will be minimal.

The bigger the meaning, the more proactive and internal motivation the coachee has. When eliciting the goal from your coachee, you want them to be getting excited about their goal. You want them feeling positive emotions. Emotions drive behaviour, and they are also connected directly to the subconscious mind.

A simple way to make goals more meaningful, is to juice up the language, with words that the coachee likes. For example, following on from the example above, the conversation could continue as follows:

> Coach: OK, so you want to be an 8/10 with your Happiness. Awesome!! By when?
> Coachee: Umm, end of the year
> Coach: Cool, what date specifically?
> Coachee: 31 December 2024
> Coach: OK, great. And for that 8/10 score, what descriptive word can you use, to spice it up a little, that 'means' 8/10 for you
> Coachee: Ummmm, I am VIBRANTLY happy by 31/12/24

Now, you've helped them to articulate their goal to be both MEASURABLE and MEANINGFUL

Achievable and Agreed – this is super important when working with a group, because if the team is not in agreeance with the goal, then achieving it will be a real challenge. And if some of the group feel it's 'impossible' to achieve, then your chances of success are slim. What you're looking for here is 100% confidence or certainty that the goal can be achieved. If you're only 50% certain of achieving the goal, then you'll achieve exactly 50% of the outcome!! Another clue is to look for congruence in your coachee or group, to ensure they are close to that 100% certainty.

Relevant and Realistic – Relevant means that the goal is aligned with your values. Is it important for you to achieve this goal? If it's not important or aligned with 'who you are', then you will really struggle to find the motivation to take action.

Realistic means is it really possible to achieve goal X, especially within a given timeframe? If your goal is to have a million dollars by tomorrow, that is probably not realistic. Mostly, you will use your common sense and feelings as to whether your goal is relevant and realistic for you. As a group, you can gauge the 'buy-in' to relevance and reality from your group's reactions and responses.

Sometimes, when you're working with your coachee, you will experience both ends of the 'realistic' spectrum where the coachee will either be:

    a. Aiming too big/high/far
    b. Not aiming big/high/far enough

Only your experience over time will determine whether you can lovingly offer them a reality check, or lovingly nudge them out of their comfort zone. Either way, work at their pace, and again, be mindful not to impose your own limitations or over-confidence.

Timely and Towards Outcome

A goal without a timeline is a wish. This is the BIGGEST mistake people have made in the past when setting up their SMART goals.

Most people, both individuals, and companies will try their best to attach a timeline, or 'by when' for their goals, but once again, they are not specific enough. They will use language such as:

- By the end of the quarter
- End of the financial year
- End of the calendar year
- End of next month
- By my birthday
- By end of 3rd quarter

Remember how the subconscious mind is like a four-year-old child? It only lives in the NOW. There is no past, future, good or bad. When we use language such as 'by the end of the quarter', the subconscious has no idea what that means. This quarter? next quarter? What's a quarter? What year? So, what happens, when you do arrive at the end of the calendar quarter, the lack of clarity simply carries the goal over to the next quarter, and the next quarter, and so on.

Getting crystal clear and specific with your goal time frame is to simply write down the exact date 'by when' you wish to achieve that goal, such as:

- By 31st March 2024
- By 31st October 2024
- By 31st December 2024
- By 30th June 2024
- By 15th November 2024
- By 30th September 2024

Also, you want to make sure your SMART goal is focusing TOWARDS your outcome. In other words, we don't focus on what we DON'T WANT, we must focus on what we DO WANT. We must use language that is present tense, positive and towards our goal.

Don't think of a pink elephant

Did you think of a pink elephant? Chances are, you probably did. Why, because that's how the subconscious mind works. It doesn't process negatives, it only hears 'think of a pink elephant'. Have you ever told your children...

Don't touch the hot stove

What do they do?? You guessed it, they touch the hot stove.

We must remove this type of language from our SMART goals:

- I don't want to be fat
- I don't want to be poor
- I don't want to be unhappy

Those statements all lead our focus on what we DON'T want, and that doesn't help move us forward.

As much as possible, we also want our SMART goal statement to be present tense. Not in the past, not in the future, but right now. Be sure to eliminate language such as:

- I want to be…
- I will achieve…
- One day I hope to…
- In the future, I will…
- Someday maybe one day

These are all future tense and will simply delay the achievement of your goal.

To summarise what is essential for our SMART gaol, and the best way to lock it in, you need:

1. Clarity
2. Focus
3. Repetition

Now that we've covered the framework for HOW to correctly structure a SMART goal, let's look at some examples together, work through them to ensure they are SMART, then it will be time for you to practice, and finally, create your own SMART goals.

Let's do a few together first. Is the following a correctly structured SMART Goal?

Goal#1 - 2 MIL USD by the end 2nd QTR

Is this a SMART Goal? Yes or No?
No, it is not, yet more than 90% of corporate goals are structured in this way. Why isn't it SMART??

1. Is that 2M USD revenue or profit? That makes an ENORMOUS difference at the end of the year.
2. End of 2nd QTR? What year? What specific date

The correctly structured SMART Goal would look like this:

✓ **We achieve 2 MIL USD profit by 30th June 2024**

You could get even more specific by substituting the 'We' to be your specific department or division. The key point is to keep it as specific AND simple as possible. Next one...

Goal#2 – We want to Increase customer satisfaction by 3%

Is it SMART? Nope. And here's why...

1. 'We want to…' pre-supposes that it will happen in the future. We don't want to achieve it in the future, we want to achieve it right now!! So be sure NOT to use phrases that are future tense. Make sure your goal statements are present tense, which will engage the subconscious mind even better.
2. 'By 3%' – increase 3% from what starting point? Is it 3% increase from 60% customer satisfaction, or from 80%, or from what? It's not clear, it's not specific. Your goal statements should be focusing **towards your outcome**, towards your final destination. So, if your current customer satisfaction is 92%, then an increase of 3% would give you a new target, a new goal, of 95% customer satisfaction.
3. By when? – there is no date given, so it will never happen!!

The correctly structured SMART Goal would be:

- ✓ **Customer Satisfaction is 95% by 20th December 2024**

Noticeably clear, outcome-focused, and as simple as possible

Goal#3 - I want to lose 5kg by August

Is it SMART? Nope. And here's why...

1. 'I want to…' pre-supposes that it will happen in the future. We don't want to achieve it in the future, we want to achieve it right now!! The subconscious mind responds best to more direct goal statements as if they're happing right now

2. 'Lose' – this language is focusing on what you don't want. Your goal statements should be focused towards your outcome, not away from what you don't want.
3. 'Lose 5kg…' – lose 5kg from what?? Losing 5kg from 60kg is OK, but losing 5kg from 200kg will hardly make a difference in your health. So again, make sure you structure your goal as a 'towards your outcome'

The correctly structured SMART Goal is:

- ✓ **Now, I am 80kg by 1ˢᵗ August 2024**

The structure of this goal pre-supposes that my start weight was 85kg, and by focusing towards my outcome, my SMART goal is structured as **I am 80kg**. It's present tense and towards the outcome. Remember, your SMART goal is like the ***final destination*** when using your google maps. If you cannot see or interpret the 'final destination' in the goal, then it needs tweaking.

Also, notice the use of the word NOW at the beginning of the statement. This is a direct command to your subconscious mind, which is like that 4-year-old kid.

I know the logical people reading this now are like "hang on Luke, you say the goal statement should say NOW, and, by 1ˢᵗ August 2024 as well? It doesn't make sense?!

What you're really saying is that "anytime, between NOW and 1ˢᵗ August 2024, I AM (not will be) 80kg." Would you like to achieve your goal Now or NOW? Of course, you want to achieve your goals sooner rather than later, so by commanding your subconscious mind with a directive NOW statement, it starts taking action and creating motivation, right now!!

In goal setting with my clients, I encourage them to use the word NOW as often as possible, and it also works for group goals as well.

Goal#4 - Get promoted by end 2024

We know it's not SMART, don't we?!
Get promoted to what?
What specific date?

> ✓ **Now, I am Managing Director by 31st December 2024**

Again, notice the use of the word NOW to command the subconscious mind, that 95% of your mind that is working towards your goal, even when you sleep!

Now it's your turn to create your own correctly structured SMART goals. Remember back to the beginning of this chapter, where you freshly wrote down all the goals you wished to achieve within one year? It's time to take those goals and write them down as SMART Goals. My suggestion is to re-write all of those 'within one-year goals' as SMART Goals. Some will be achieved within two months, some six months, and some twelve months, so be sure to write the exact date you wish to achieve them. Here is another blank page, so go ahead, and write down your correctly structured SMART goals, NOW…

Great! How does that feel? Most likely, you feel clearer, more motivated and inspired. Some of you may even wish to write down MORE goals, which is totally OK.

When working with your clients, once they've correctly structured their SMART goal, you can ask them:

"On a scale of 1-10, how confident do you feel, that you can achieve this Goal?"

The answer you're looking for is 10/10 or 100% confident. Anything less, and there is a high probability they WON'T achieve their goal. If they are just 50% confident or certain to achieve their goal, how much of their goal do you think they'll achieve? That's right, exactly 50%. So, you need to increase their level of confidence and certainty. A few ways to do that…

1. Ask them 'What would need to happen to get it from 50% to 100% confident?'. Answers may include something about their limiting beliefs, that they need to complete the full action plan, etc. Whatever they say, is correct for them, and as their coach, you must support them to get to 100% certainty

2. Get them to 'lock in' their goal, by repeating a mini mantra. In other words, have them say their goal, out loud, repeatedly, for three to five minutes. The more intense they do this, the more they will remember the goal. Challenge them, push them, support them

3. Focus and Repetition – the goal will never be locked into their subconscious mind if they don't focus on it DAILY, and REPEATEDLY. They should post their goal somewhere they can see them, every day. They should continue to repeat it out loud, further locking into their neurology. The

deeper they lock it in, the greater the subconscious mind will support them in achieving their goal.

At the end of each year, Coach Cristy and I sit down and evaluate our goals from the current year, and then plan our goals for the next year. We usually end up with a list of seventy or so SMART Goals that we wish to achieve within the next twelve months. Some we consciously take action on, while others we leave to our subconscious mind to achieve them. We then review the goals every three months. Some we achieve, some we change, some we delete, and sometimes we add new ones. The point here is that your goals are not set in stone. You need to be flexible with the direction your Life and Business is going. If a goal is no longer relevant to you, let it go. If you didn't yet achieve your goal, amend it. If you have a new fresh goal that excites you, add it. At the end of the year, when we review our goals, we have achieved at least 50% of all those goals we wrote down, simply as a SMART Goal. That means we achieved 35 goals within a year. Is that good? Only you know what's good for you. For us, we feel great because most of those goals are achieved with minimal effort. In other words, do not underestimate the power of a correctly structured SMART goal.

To summarise, you want to maximize your SMART Goal by:

1. Clarity – following the structure outlined above, for correct SMART goal setting
2. Focus – remind yourself daily and often
3. Repetition – remind yourself repeatedly, using a mantra or similar

To embed the goal even deeper into the subconscious mind, you can create what is called a vision board. A vision board is unique in that it 'speaks the language' of the subconscious mind, which is:

1. Images
2. Emotions

All you need to do is find images that relate to the main goals you wish to achieve. You can cut them out from magazines, or you can create them digitally. Search for some vision board examples on google to get the idea. Next, create a single slide PowerPoint, find images related to your goal on google that evoke positive emotions, save those, and add them to your PowerPoint. Remember to choose an image that reminds you of your goal, and when you look at it, it stirs up positive emotions, such as motivation, confidence, wow, etc. Then, you just arrange the images how you like, and you save that PowerPoint as a JPEG file. You can then use that as a screen saver on your PC or phone, or get it printed into a large poster that you place somewhere you see every day.

On a scale of 1-10, how important is it to correctly structure your SMART goal, and lock it into your subconscious mind?? That's right, 15 out of 10. If your client is not clear on their goal, they'll never achieve it, and neither will you!!

We've spent quite a bit of time focusing on correctly structured SMART goals, and the reasons are important. Typical human tendency is to focus on problems. Neuroscience tells us that on average, 70% of our thoughts are negative. We think about our problems, talk about our problems, replay the problems in our mind, and we are essentially problem focused.

> **Oftentimes, the problem is not the problem, it's the thinking about the problem that is the problem**

In addition to being problem-focused, we layer problems one on top of the other. In fact, we layer multiple problems, all at once, which is why it's easy to feel overwhelmed or stuck. The 'simplest' of problems or challenges, get rolled up into our bigger problems, making it feel impossible to solve and hard to navigate a way forward.

This is why the creation and elicitation of the SMART goal are so important. It's like a 'lighthouse', that beacon of light that directs our focus away from the problem, towards the solution, towards what we want.

Awareness and Action: Get together with a friend or colleague, and help them to create a SMART goal, following the steps outlined above. Be sure not to TELL them their goal, as your Coachee should always, always, always, choose their own goal. Be mindful that you don't tell them to 'make it SMART', as they will not have learned this process yet. Simply ask them questions, to elicit their goal. Here is an example of a typical SMART goal elicitation conversation:

Coachee: I want to lose 5kg
Coach: OK, great, you'd like to lose 5kg. May I ask, what is your current weight?

Coachee: currently, right now, I'm 85kg
Coach: OK, thanks for sharing. So, if you'd like to lose 5kg, what would be your final, target weight?

Coachee: Well, 85kg minus 5kg, is 80kg. I would like to be 80kg
Coach: OK great!! And by when, what date, would you like to be 80kg?

Coachee: I would like to be 80kg by the end of the year
Coach: 80kg by the end of the year. What year would that be (it's OK to have a sense of humour). What date specifically

Coachee: I would like to be 80kg by 31/12/2022
Coach: Nice!! And how could you make your goal statement more present tense, as if it's happening right now??

Coachee: Ummm, what do you mean coach?
Coach: When you say, 'I would like to be', it's throwing your goal

into the future. What words or language could you use, to make it more present tense??

Coachee: Now, I am 80kg by 31/12/2022
Coach: Great!! Say it again, please!

Coachee: Now, I am 80kg by 31/12/2022
Coach: Great!! Say it one more time please, a little louder (get them to repeat a few times until it's congruent. You will see a shift in their body language. You want them to OWN their goal)

Coachee: NOW, I AM 80kg by 31/12/2022
Coach: Great job!! How does that feel in your body?
Coachee: Wow, amazing, it feels great. I feel much more confident that I can achieve it
Coach: Well done, and congratulations on creating such a clear, powerful goal 😊

With a correctly structured SMART goal, you or your coachee are already 50% more likely to achieve it. Feel free to practice this exercise on a few different goals, with a few different people. You need to be able to effortlessly elicit goals from anyone, on any topic, to be an effective coach.

It's important to reiterate here, that whatever framework or style of coaching that you utilize, it's really REALLY important to support your coachee to clearly articulate their SMART Goal. With a well defined, correctly structured SMART goal, your coachee becomes so CLEAR that the action planning steps will be much more powerful and effective, helping them INSTANTLY to achieve IMPACT in their lives and work.

Now that you've practiced a few times, you're ready to explore the full power of the POW Coaching Model!

CHAPTER 6
POW Coaching Model Overview

"Coaching is about asking questions to help people find their own answers."

— Zain Asher

Very simply, POW is an acronym for:

P = Problem/Challenge
O = Outcome
W = Way Forward

The POW Coaching Model was created by Coach Cristy and myself through a combination of the following:

a. The needs shared by Executives and Leaders wanting to implement a coaching culture. They wanted to solve their two biggest coaching-related problems:
   1. "We don't have time to Coach" – they needed to overcome this resistance in both coach and coachee, by shortening sessions to less than thirty minutes
   2. Not having a simple coaching framework that could be taught to Leaders, that would support the implementation of a coaching culture

b. Hands-on practical knowledge from our thousands of hours of real-life Leadership Coaching experience

c. Inspiration from thought leaders such as Marshall Goldsmith and David Allen, among many others

The POW Coaching model finally crystallized through the creation of our 65hr Leadership Coaching Certification. We'd already created a longer, more in-depth coaching model called the GROWTH Coaching Model, which is ideal for longer conversations of twenty to sixty minutes. We wanted to add an additional coaching model, something shorter and more direct, to help those Leaders and Executives, to have meaningful coaching conversations in less than twenty minutes. We wanted to create instant impact.

One day, after a very successful Strategic Alignment workshop with a large MNC company, I suddenly realized that I was really good at helping Leaders shift their focus from problems towards solutions.

Typically, in a Strategic Alignment session, there are roughly eight to fifteen senior Leaders in the room. I ask them to write down all the problems or challenges they perceive on a piece of paper. They do this by themselves first, and I give them around three minutes to 'empty their heads'.

Then, they are invited over to the flip chart, share their problems/challenges with the small group (four to five people) and then consolidate their challenges onto the flip chart. The final step is to get them to 'agree' on the top three to four challenges.

After teaching them how to correctly structure a SMART goal, just as we did in the previous chapter, I'd invite them back to their respective flipcharts, choose their number 1 challenge, and write at the top of a fresh page.

I'd then explain the process called FLIPPING, which is essentially flipping that problem or challenge 180 degrees towards a solution, towards a correctly structured SMART goal. The golden question I ask to help them shift their focus from problem to solution is:

> "With this problem/challenge you've just identified, what goal do you need to achieve, that if you DID achieve, the problem would disappear"

I'd been using this FLIPPING process for a couple of years, with amazing results. After they clearly identified their SMART goal, they would then continue with more brainstorming, prioritizing, and developing a detailed action plan.

The final piece of the puzzle in developing the POW Coaching Model was after reading David Allens 'Getting Things Done', which is an amazing, practical guide for effective time management. He shares his concept of the 'very next physical action' to help people keep moving forward. And thus, the POW Coaching Model was born:

P = Problem/Challenge – help your coachee to CLEARLY identify ONE problem or challenge, in one sentence

O = Outcome - What outcome (SMART Goal) do they wish to achieve, the achievement of which, the problem ceases to exist

W = Way Forward – What are the very next (2-3) physical actions

Since its inception, the POW Coaching Model has been taught to over one-thousand Leaders all around the world, with great success. It has helped dozens of organizations effectively implement a Coaching Culture that actually works. It's the most powerful, effective, and practical Leadership Coaching Model that I'm aware of. In short, it helps Leaders to achieve Instant Impact.

With practice, you can conduct what we call conversational coaching, meaning that it can be a very informal process of helping your colleagues solve their problems, with conversations at the water cooler, coffee machine, or lunch break. It can also be used in more formal settings such as performance reviews, pitstops, or feedback sessions.

It's also a very powerful self-coaching tool. Whenever you feel stuck on a particular project or problem, you can guide yourself through the same POW process, to help get unstuck, overcome procrastination, and keep moving forward.

Listed below are some of the most common times Leaders have effectively used the POW Coaching Model, for instant impact:

- Supporting subordinates to solve their own problems
- Helping colleagues to get 'unstuck'
- Brainstorming sessions, individual or group
- Action planning and KPI development
- As part of delivering effective feedback
- Project work, ideation and innovation sessions
- Personal problems that have been brought to the 'office'
- Anytime there is an opportunity to empower your team

Remember, you can also use this same framework with yourself and your own problems and challenges. It's a brilliant way to overcome procrastination.

Awareness and Action: Practice the FLIPPING process, by identifying a challenge or problem by ASKING questions to the coachee or group. Then, help them identify the SMART Goal, that if you COULD achieve it, the problem would disappear. This is super effective when eliciting problems/challenges in a team setting. It's a good 'muscle' to start practicing now, even before the full implementation of the POW Coaching Model. With practice, you will almost instantly be able to flip a problem towards a solution. As you can imagine, that is GREAT for you and your organization. The impact is massive. Here are a few examples:

Problem: I'm too fat
Outcome: Now, I am 80kg by the 1st August 2024

Problem: I'm not confident enough
Outcome: Now, I am passionately confident in public speaking by 1st December 2024

Good luck with your Flipping practice!

Let's explore each segment of the POW Coaching Model in more detail.

CHAPTER 7
P = Problem. Clearly identifying the Problem/Challenge

"A problem well stated is a problem half solved."
— Charles Kettering

Your job here is to help your coachee to identify ONE problem or challenge in one clear sentence.

Remember, one of the key points of utilizing the POW Coaching Model is to help our Coachee shift their focus from problem/negative focus to solution/positive focus. To do that effectively, we must clearly identify what the problem is. We need to acknowledge the truth of the situation, without getting lost in hours of 'problem focus'.

Before opening any coaching conversation, you want to ensure you have rapport and trust with your coachee. If there is no trust, they won't open up, and it will be a very surface-level conversation. Rapport is an ongoing process with your peers and subordinates. Just because you have it once, does not mean you have it forever. Also, just because you have the title of 'boss', does not automatically grant you the trust, respect, and rapport you think you deserve. Very important too, is no judgment or ridicule. What may seem like an 'easy' problem for you to solve, maybe a huge challenge for your coachee. Practice your generous listening and do your best to be totally present.

Once the trust is established, some of the easiest coaching conversation starters you can utilize are:

> "What's on your mind today"
>
> "What would you like to explore today"
>
> "Please tell me about the situation"
>
> "Tell me more…" (this is best used when your coachee has already launched into the problem that they are experiencing)

If related to a project or task, you can start by focusing on what worked well, then followed by what could be improved. For example:

> "What worked well in the project? (Let them share, then). What challenges did you have?"
>
> "What success did you have? (Let them share, then). What could be improved for next time?"

Of course, there are dozens of variations on these above conversation starters, many of which you can adjust, depending on the situation. Your practice and experience will lead you to some 'favourite' questions to ask, to get things started.

When eliciting the problem, we need to be as time efficient as possible, yet give the process all the time it needs. We do not want to make assumptions about what we think the problem might be, which is a common trap when you are coaching your subordinates.

At the same time, you need to be guiding the conversation, to ensure you can get the problem statement very clearly, before moving on to the next steps.

Sometimes, identifying the challenge or problem is super obvious, very quick, and very easy, taking perhaps just one or two minutes. Other times, it may take you some time to fully elicit one clear problem.

Remember, one problem, one solution per coaching conversation.

There are a few reasons why the problem elicitation may take longer:

a. **Your coachee just needs to vent** - Being in a Leadership role is not always easy. When solving problem after problem for the organization, your own personal problems (work or life-related) begin piling up. Most of the time, that Leader doesn't have anyone to share their burdens with. They can't be talking about their problems with the big boss, as their boss wants to hear solutions. They can't really tell their subordinates, as it may come across as blaming or complaining. Their peers are not always available, and their life partners don't really want to hear about *another* problem at work.
It can be very beneficial to allow your coachee to vent. Be sure to maintain your presence, listen actively, and as always, be non-judgemental. You'll normally find that after 5-7 minutes, they'll exhale deeply, look at you, and say 'thank you'.

This venting process could last for up to fifteen minutes, so as the Coach, you want to keep the process moving forward and try to limit the venting to five to seven minutes. If you feel the venting is dragging on too long, you can politely interrupt, and use one of the following 'pattern interrupt' questions:

"OK great, so can you please summarise the problem in one sentence?"

"OK got it, thanks for sharing. What is the core challenge you'd like to discuss today?"

"Can you bottom-line the situation for me in one sentence?"

One of the biggest benefits of teaching the POW Coaching Model to a group of Leaders within an organization, is that we create a safe space for them to openly vent and be 'heard', by their peers. Their peers 'get it' and can understand their frustrations and problems at a deeper level. This means that during their practice coaching conversations, not only are they developing their coaching skills, but they also get to solve some of their real-world problems and challenges

   b. **Vagueness** – Some people find it very difficult to clearly articulate their problems. This could be because they are layering their problems (more on that below) or that they are not the best communicator and have challenges in articulating their thoughts and words. It could also be that they are trying to communicate in their non-native language, or even certain cultural 'limitations' about not openly expressing themselves in a certain way. For example, in many Asian countries, 'problems' are sometimes not openly discussed for the fear of 'losing face'. In other cultures, especially organizational cultures (not limited to country or location) there may be a toxic work environment, with no psychological safety. When team members talk about problems or mistakes, they are openly criticized, judged, or humiliated, and so for those reasons, it's simply safer to NOT say anything.

Whatever the reasons, you as the Coach need to employ your rapport, and your empathy, and create an environment of Psychological Safety. You can reassure your coachee, that your discussion will remain totally confidential. You will practice your patience, and your will ensure your presence, by removing any distractions. Remember pacing and leading? You will want to move at the pace of your coachee, encouraging them gently to open up, dig deeper, and gain more clarity. To get beyond the vagueness and get more specific, here are a few questions you can ask:

"Please tell me more..."
"Who/What/How/When specifically..."
"What do you mean by that..."
"How is that a problem..."
"If you could summarise the problem in one sentence, what would that sound like"

An empowering way to show your empathy is through active listening, and gentle encouragement. Statements such as 'thank you for sharing' or 'thanks for being so open' are great ways to build deeper trust and give them some positive reinforcement that it's OK to share what going on inside their mind.

As you continue to practice this POW Coaching Model with your subordinates, you are helping them be a better communicator. You're helping them articulate their thoughts more clearly, and you're helping them to openly express themselves more, when dealing with challenges, having concerns, or wanting to share ideas. This ultimately leads to them becoming better problem solvers as well. Through the process of POW, they are learning the process of POW as well, so you're giving them a structure to move from Problem to Solution to Action.

c. **The layering of problems** - As humans, we tend to layer our problems one on top of the other, on top of the other, creating a big, entangled mess of problems. Being respectful to allow them a little space for sharing and venting, you still want to help them identify the most important problem for today's conversation and keep the conversation moving forward. One problem, one Solution.

When you begin to hear multiple problems being shared during the 'venting', when your coachee finally pauses for a breath, you simply clarify with them, the most important problem for today's conversation. For example:

Coach: "Thank you for sharing. I'm hearing you mention three situations at the moment, that are challenging for you:

i. Your son is struggling with their grades
ii. Your subordinate Mary is under-performing
iii. You feel that you don't have any work-life balance
Which one of those is most important to talk about today?"

Coachee: "Well, I suppose that it's Mary's under-performance because it's actually causing me a lot of stress"

From this point here, you can ask the coachee to tell you a little more about the situation, to create more clarity, such as

"Tell me more about Mary's under-performance"

Or, if it is relatively clear, you could ask them to clarify the problem statement in one clear sentence. Their response may simply be:

"Mary is not achieving her KPI for the last three months, and has an unwilling attitude"

Again, you definitely want to practice your patience and empathy here, as these problems have a certain 'weight' that burden a lot of people. Helping them to separate these problems into individual items is so liberating for your coachee. The instant impact has begun!

This step, done correctly, helps them be up to 50% of the way to solving the problem, by being able to clearly articulate the one problem they wish to resolve, in today's conversation. Do they have another problem they wish to resolve? Great!! Just schedule another coaching conversation with them.

It is also important during this part of POW that you allow your coachee to decide which problem to focus on. They may be short-term or long-term, they may seem big or small, and they may seem insignificant or minuscule. However they present their problem, it's your job to support them to identify that one challenge, that if they could move forward on, would help them be more 'free', more productive, and more confident.

One other challenge you may experience, as the Coach, in eliciting a challenge or problem from your coachee, is that as you try to get a conversation going, or you try to elicit their challenge, they say:

"Hmmm, nothing. No real challenges"

Now that may be true, and it may not necessarily be true. At this point, one thing to remember is that Coaching is a leadership tool.

Based on your years of leadership experience, you will have gathered many leadership tools and techniques to effectively lead your team. The truth is that you cannot coach all of the people all of the time. It's a situational tool that is best used at the right time. If you are experiencing heavy 'resistance' from your coachee, as you try to initiate a coaching conversation, it simply may not be the best time. In these instances, you may be better off:

- Giving direct feedback, using the BIFF Feedback model, or similar
- Scheduling a coaching conversation in the near future, at a more appropriate time
- Telling or directing their actions, to be more efficient with time
- Engage in a Mentoring conversation
- Disciplinary action, as necessary

Giving direct feedback is often the best place to start, with a highly resistant subordinate coachee. Following the BIFF model is one of the easiest and most effective feedback models to use. Especially with the final step (F = Future) as that becomes a pure coaching conversation. In summary:

B = Behaviour
I = Impact
F = Feeling
F = Future

Before starting any feedback conversation, it's best to seek permission first, to ensure psychological safety, and to ensure a more direct and efficient conversation. You can ask permission with one of the example openers below:

"Hi Frank, do you have a few minutes for a straight talk"

"Hi Frank, may I openly share some feedback with you"

"Hi Frank, can we have an open and direct conversation for a few minutes"

99% of the time, Frank says 'yeah, sure'. They are now much more open to hearing and receiving what you have to say, and you've set the scene for what is about to happen. In the rare instances that they say 'no', simply ask them "when would be a good time", agree on that date and time, and lock it in the calendar.

Behaviour - What behaviour have you observed? What are they doing or not doing? Stick to facts and data, not opinions, gossip, or feeling

Impact – What impact is their behaviour having on you, the team, the organization, or the customer. Once again, stick to the facts, to prevent denial or reasoning of the situation

Feeling – openly express how this makes you feel. Frustrated, angry, concerned, etc. As humans, we can relate to feelings, so it can give some scale to the issue. Side note – most feedback sessions are a train wreck, as they normally start with a charged emotion such as anger or frustration. By following the BIFF model, you are opening with fact, logic, and observable behaviour. As you follow the process, at this point, it is OK to share your feelings

Future – this is where you get to put your Coaching hat on. In essence, you've already covered the Problem section of POW above. Now it's time to shift the focus towards the future and solution. A couple of things need to happen in this step:

- be sure to share a clear vision of your expectations. Don't assume they should know the 'correct' behaviour. Share that with them openly, and ensure they understand

- Help them elicit the correct behavioural outcome as a SMART Goal (Outcome in POW)
- Ask them (don't tell them) what specific actions they will take, to improve their behaviour or performance (Way Forward)
- As you summarise the actions, be sure to ask, "What support do you need?"

When facilitating feedback in this way, especially by finishing with the agreed-upon actions with 'by when' dates and milestones, you are helping the coachee be more accountable and responsible for their actions. They will be more likely to improve. Be sure to follow up as necessary and support them with the changes they've agreed.

You don't want to 'force' your coaching conversations onto your subordinates. Ensure they flow naturally as you can, schedule them regularly to build them in as part of your leadership function and let your coachee decide their outcomes and focus areas.

> **In summary, your job here during the P section of POW, is to help your coachee to identify ONE problem or challenge in one clear sentence.**

Now that the problem or challenge is clearly identified, you need to support your coachee to shift their focus, towards a positive Outcome...

Awareness and Action: Practice delivering the BIFF Feedback Model to one of your subordinates or peers

CHAPTER 8
O = Outcome. Shifting focus towards a crystal-clear SMART Goal

> *"To conquer frustration, one must remain intensely focused on the outcome, not the obstacles"*
> – T.F. Hodge

Your job here, is to support your Coachee to come up with a one-sentence SMART Goal, that represents their Outcome, the achievement of which, the Problem ceases to exist.

During this step, you're helping your coachee shift their focus from problem to solution

The good news here is that you've already learned how to correctly structure a SMART Goal, so it's time to put your skills into practice with your coachee.

Once your coachee has clearly identified their ONE challenge/problem in ONE clear sentence, you'll want a nice clean transition that helps them shift their focus from the problem, towards a solution. Here are some elegant examples:

- what would be your preferred outcome

- what would you like instead
- What would be the ideal scenario
- If you had a magic wand, what would you prefer

Because of human our nature to focus on problems, your coachee may not initially 'get' this line of questioning, so you may need to patiently, lovingly repeat the question, to ensure they understand. A couple of ways to do that...

> Coach: Well, if this is the challenge <repeat challenge clearly>, then what would be your preferred outcome

> Coach: A moment ago, you shared that <repeat challenge clearly>, so what would be your ideal scenario

The key here is your patience and maintaining your non-judgemental attitude. If they haven't experienced coaching before and/or haven't correctly structured SMART goals before, they are stepping outside of their comfort zone into the unknown. Guide them gently and support them to express their desired outcome.

Once they've expressed themselves, you can also clarify by asking something similar to the below:

> Coach: So, if you were to achieve <repeat their outcome>, then the problem would disappear?

> Coach: If I understand correctly if you achieve <their outcome>, then the problem would cease to exist, is that correct?

At this point, they should smile and exclaim "Yeah!!"

Most likely though, their outcome is not yet articulated as a SMART Goal. You will need to continue your gentle questioning, to help them make it SMART. Help them to get more specific. If it's an 'intangible' goal such as happiness or confidence, you can use those scaling questions we mentioned earlier. If you are not clear, simply ask more questions to create greater clarity, for both you and for them. And be sure to ALWAYS ask, by when, and get that specific date. Not an end-of-month, end-of-quarter, end-of-year time frame.

Please also remember that MOST people do NOT know how to correctly structure a SMART goal, so you will continue to ask questions, until you've fully elicited a SMART goal from them.

Here is an extended example, starting from the transition from P to O

> Coach: Thank you for sharing. So, what I'm hearing is that you don't have enough work-life balance, is that correct?
>
> Coachee: Yes, that's correct
> Coach: OK, and on a scale of 1-10, with 1 being horrible and 10 being amazing, how would you rate your current work-life balance
>
> Coachee: Hmm, I'd say it's a 5 out of 10
> Coach: OK, so in an ideal scenario, what would you prefer your work-life balance to be?
>
> Coachee: Well, I'd like it to be a 10, but I think that's unrealistic right now, so I'd like to aim for an 8
> Coach: An 8/10 work-life balance, is that correct?
>
> Coachee: Yes, correct

Coach: And by when would you like to have an 8/10 work-life balance?

Coachee: End of the year
Coach: What date specifically?

Coachee: 31st December 2024
Coach: OK, good. Can you kindly repeat your outcome in one sentence, please

Coachee: Now, my work-life balance is an 8/10 by 31/12/2022
Coach: Nice!! And what kind of descriptive word could you use, that *means* 8/10 for you?

Let them think. When your coachee stares off into space, it's a good thing. Never disturb them. Whatever descriptive word they come up, is good for them. They should be motivated and inspired.

Coachee: Flow!! Yes, Flow!!!
Coach: Great, so repeat in full, one more time, please
Coachee: Now, my work-life balance FLOWS by 31/12/2024
Coach: Amazing, well done (get them to repeat a few times, to fully lock it into their neurology)

Remember, you're looking for congruency, confidence, and certainty at this point. The more confident they are, the more likely they are to achieve their goal.

In coaching conversations, this outcome focus with the clear elicitation of a SMART goal is often overlooked. The coachee may briefly hint towards an outcome, yet, because most of us are working in fast-paced organizations, our natural tendency is to jump straight from the Problem statement, directly into the action planning. That's like your google maps trying to calculate a route to a vague destination. You'll get lost!!

It's the same with their action planning or way forward. If the goal is not crystal clear, the following brainstorming and action planning will be wishy-washy. Chances are, they'll come up with the same actions they've taken before, which have NOT helped them solve their problem or achieve their goal

As the coach, you must be very aware to help your coachee clearly articulate their Outcome as a SMART goal FIRST, before jumping into the actions. They will tend to jump to the actions too quickly, so you'll need gently 'reel them back' to articulate their SMART goal first. With a clearer outcome, the quality and impact of their actions will be much greater, and the likelihood of success massively improved.

Chances are, you are also a great problem solver, that's why you are a great Leader. In your head, once the problem is clearly identified, you will ALSO have the natural tendency to jump straight into brainstorming and action planning, so be mindful of this habit. It's not your job to solve your coachees problem. This is the biggest trap new coaches make. You feel the necessity to take on the burden of the results. It's not yours to carry. The best gift you can give your coachee is following the process of POW and allowing them to do the heavy lifting. You do not need to be an expert in the problem area that the coachee has presented. In fact, it's often easier, as the Coach, to know nothing about the problem or solution. Why? Because you won't have the urge to TELL THEM how to fix it.

When we know the challenges and solutions intimately, within a certain context (such as a department or division), or when that 'thing' has happened to us in the past, we really must resist the urge to tell them what to do. Because we've solved it before, our tendency will be to tell them. Please resist that urge to tell them, which will be for all three steps of POW...

With the Problem – resist the urge to assume and summarise for them

With the Outcome – don't skip it, let them articulate it, in their words, and make it SMART

With the Way Forward – let THEM brainstorm, prioritize and decide which actions to take

This will be YOUR biggest challenge in the beginning. If you are telling them what to do in any of the three steps, then it's the way you've always been doing it. Patience is your friend. Bite your tongue, sit on your hands, and do whatever you need to do, and overcome that urge to tell them or fix it right now.

In summary, your job here during the O section of POW, is to help your coachee to identify a SMART Outcome, the achievement of which, the problem ceases to exist

Now, the initial problem/challenge has been clearly identified, and you've helped them articulate a SMART goal that focuses towards their preferred outcome, you are ready to help them create the Way Forward...

Awareness and Action: Practice flipping as many problem statements as you can, into a SMART Goal. Start with a list of twenty challenges, and create the SMART Goal, the achievement of which, the problem ceases to exist

CHAPTER 9
W = Way Forward. What are the very next physical actions

"Words may inspire, but only action creates Change"
– Simon Sinek

Your job here is to help your coachee identify two or three physical actions, that they can take asap.

Physical action means to actually do something. 'Thinking about it' is not a physical action. 'Reflecting upon it' is not a physical action. 'Wishing for it' is not a physical action. You must support your coachee to come up with some actions they can take, that lead them closer to their goal.

One of the reasons the POW Coaching Model is so powerful is that you are breaking down what initially may seem like a big goal with huge actions into smaller more manageable pieces. This helps your coachee overcome procrastination and overwhelm. Here is a serious question for all the adults in the room…

"How do you eat an Elephant?"

The correct answer is **"One bite at a time"**

The elephant, of course, is that BIG goal. Any goal, no matter its size, is simply achieved with one action at a time, one step at a time, one bite at a time. The bigger the goal, the more steps, yet the process is the same.

That's what you're doing here. You're helping your coachee break down the goal into small bite-sized chunks. Those first two or three initial steps help them get unstuck and get them moving forward. With each action that they take, they are one step closer to their goal. Then, with each additional action that they take, they feel more confident, they are building momentum, and they feel more certain they can achieve it.

You will need a nice transition question here, as you did when you transitioned between Problem and Outcome. You want a nice, clean break between each segment, yet it should feel seamless and conversational. Once you've helped them elicit their SMART Goal outcome, and you've had them repeat it a few times for full ownership, you can ask one of the following transition questions to begin the Way Forward Process…

- What are some actions you can take, to achieve your goal
- What can you do, to achieve your goal
- What needs to happen, to achieve your goal
- What action have you not tried yet

Basically, at the beginning here, you are facilitating a mini brainstorm with your coachee. Be sure to elicit as many as you can, by simply repeating 'anything else' or 'what else' or 'is there something else you can do'. Allow them the time and space, as they stare off into the distance, to gather their thoughts and consider their actions. Encourage and acknowledge everything that they share. Once you've elicited three to six actions, you can ask them to prioritize their top two actions. Some good questions here are:

- With these actions that you've listed, which one is most important
- From this list of xx actions, which one is the highest priority
- Which of these actions is most important

You're helping them trim down their list to the two most important actions.

Then, you need to ensure that it's the very next physical action. Often, with action planning, the action step that the coachee comes up with is still too big and/or complicated. In other words, there are still a few sub-steps involved to complete it. This can result in procrastination or overwhelm, resulting in the coachee NOT taking action. You'll want to break it down into really small parts.

For example, if we work with the goal statement from the previous example:

Now, I am 80kg by 31/12/2024

Perhaps the coachee came up with the following actions:

- More exercise
- Better portion control for food
- Drink more water
- Stop drinking beer
- Go to bed earlier

As you can see, most of these actions are still very vague, and not specific at all. However, for now, you'll help them prioritize to their top 2, and let's say they choose:

1. More exercise
2. Stop drinking beer

These are not yet 'very next physical actions'. They are more like an idea than an action.

In this very important part of the Way Forward, you will want to 'chunk down' and get very clear on HOW specifically they will take those actions, and BY WHEN will they complete those intended actions. By focusing on the highest priority first, your next line of questioning could be:

- How specifically will you do more exercise
- What specific exercise will you do
- How often and for what duration will you do that exercise

Often, your coachee will remain vague or not clear enough, so you must help them drill down. This is not about micro-managing or being a 'policeman', this is about creating clarity and helping them be more responsible and accountable for their actions. Here is an example of how this conversation might continue:

> Coachee: Well, I could go for a thirty-minute walk three times a week. And I'd also like to do some yoga three times a week
> Coach: Sounds great! Focusing on walking first, when is the best time for you to go walking, and where is good for you?
>
> Coachee: Definitely in the mornings for me, as evenings are busy with other commitments. I have a couple of nice parks nearby to my house, with a few different ways to get to them, so there is a good variety for me to choose from, to keep it interesting
> Coach: Sounds nice. And what time in the morning will you go for these walks?

Coachee: Well, my alarm normally goes off at 600am, but I've been dozing and hitting snooze a lot lately, and then I check out social media for a while. I think it's best for me if I go for the walk, after getting straight up at 600am
Coach: And how will you keep yourself accountable (or remind yourself) to do that?

Coachee: Ummm, my partner is an early bird and is up from 530am, so I could ask them to nudge me and make sure I actually get up, get dressed, and get out the door…lol
Coach: Great, sounds like a plan. And when will you speak to your partner?

Coachee: I'll speak to them tonight and ask for their support.
Coach: Great. Earlier, you mentioned going for a walk three times per week. Do you have a preference for what days that would be?

Coachee: Hmmm, good question. Not Mondays, because they just seem a little busier, so maybe Tuesday, Thursday, and a longer walk on Saturdays
Coach: Great!! Anything else you need to do, to keep your commitment to walking three times per week

Coachee: Well, I could put that walking schedule into my calendar, so I see it throughout the day, anytime I'm updating my calendar. That will help keep me focused
Coach: OK, anything else?

Coachee: Umm, nope, I think that's it

Coach: OK, good job. Can you kindly summarise your actions steps for more exercise:

Coachee: I will walk 3 times per week, on Tuesdays, Thursdays, and Saturdays, first thing in the morning after I wake up. My partner will support me, and I'll speak to them tonight, and I will update my calendar for the walking schedule
Coach: Outstanding. Final question…when will you start?

Coachee: Tomorrow morning 😊
Coach: Amazing!!

You would then repeat the same process for the SPECIFICS on their yoga exercise plan, for the 3 times per week.

Once you're clear on the mini action plan for their exercise (walking and yoga), you can then explore their desire to stop drinking beer. In the same process…you'll create some clarity, ask questions, dig deeper, and come up with a specific action plan.

As you break the bigger/vague actions down to their very next physical action components, it creates massive clarity for the coachee, and the steps themselves are often SUPER easy. Typically, many of the very next physical actions are quite basic and really easy to execute. Often, they'll be:

- Enter it into my calendar
- Email that person
- Send that person a text
- Send a meeting invitation to the people concerned
- Do 5-10min research
- Speak to that person

- Set a reminder to my calendar/post-it note/fridge door
- Ask for help or support
- Just do it

As additional support for your coachee, if the actions they've decided takes less than one minute, such as entering a reminder or recurring event into their calendar, have them do it right NOW, inside of the coaching conversation. That is now one action that they have already completed! That is instant impact!! The momentum builds right away. Once they've completed that action, you could simply respond "which action next?"

Your real purpose here is to help your coachee break the bigger action step down into smaller physical actions, that can be easily done. When working with leaders, they may decide to just do those actions themselves, or they may choose to delegate some of the action steps you've helped them identify.

When working with your direct reports and subordinates, you may vary the depth or detail that you get into, with this Way Forward process. If you have a subordinate that has 'challenges' completing their tasking, or is late with completing things on time, then you will probably want to drill down much deeper and get very very specific on their actions and 'by whens'. When working with other subordinates, who have a good track record for completing what they say they will complete, then you may not need to drill down so deep. Be flexible, and adaptable to the needs of your coachee.

It's usually good practice to also ask your coachee to repeat back any actions they've decided, along with their 'by whens'. This helps them take greater accountability and responsibility for the actions that THEY decided. Generally, it's a very good sign if your coachee is taking notes, although this is not always necessary, and you shouldn't really 'force' them to take notes. Again though, if there is a history of them not completing tasks on time, then it might be useful to nudge them a little stronger.

By now, you are almost ready to wrap up the coaching conversation, so you'll want a nice 'closer' to finish it off smoothly. Once the coachee has recapped their actions, a couple of nice questions to ask could be:

- How do you feel about our conversation today?
- How do you feel now (good to ask if they were stressed or frustrated at the beginning)
- What new awareness do you have about yourself and/or the situation today?

Listen carefully to whatever they say. As always, encourage, congratulate, and acknowledge their efforts, so that they have a positive overall experience from the coaching conversation, which will help make them more open and willing next time. For the final question, please ensure to ask:

- Is there any support or resources you need from me

Again, listen carefully, if they do request further support or assistance, and communicate directly with them if you can commit to their request. If you say you will help them in a specific way, be sure to do so. That additional help, support, or guidance can come in many forms, such as:

- sending them that report
- sending them a link or file to access information
- speaking to someone on their behalf
- Having a 'word' to the other department
- Setting up that meeting
- lending them a book
- checking in on them, as requested/required
- Asking to schedule your next coaching conversation with them

Set your own calendar reminders, that will remind you to follow up or complete that support action for them, as you agreed. It sets a great example when you make it important to complete any support requests.

Whether they asked for help or replied 'thanks, I'm good now', the most elegant way to fully complete the session, is to simply say:

> "Thank you very much, and looking forward to chatting again soon"

When the conversation is complete, be sure to consolidate your own notes, in whatever way works for you. Whether you use a diary, a file, or digitally, however you do it, be sure to capture the actions they agreed to take, with 'by whens', in some manner. Especially at the beginning, if you are new to coaching your teams. Also be sure to complete any tasks that you agreed to take, with the best practice of doing those asap. You don't want them coming back to you and saying, 'oh hey, did you do that thing for me yet?'. For longer-term actions or follow-ups, be sure to set your own reminders into your calendar, to ensure you complete them promptly.

One quick word of caution...at the end of many coaching conversations, I've heard new coaches ask...

> "Is there anything else you'd like to discuss today"

This is a trap. You don't want to get started on a new topic/challenge/problem, instead, you want a nice clean and clear closure. Simply say thank you and close the conversation.

Included below is a POW Coaching Model template that will help you in the beginning, to keep with the flow of the process. In reality, you'll probably only need to use this two or three times, after which, it will be embedded in your mind and communication as an easy process for you to follow and replicate. Here's the template:

POW Coaching Model

DATE:
COACHEE:

P	• what is on your mind • what would you like to explore • tell me about the situation • bottom line it for me • tell me about it in one sentence	
	Be sure to focus on ONE problem or challenge at a time	
	• Im hearing probA, probB, probC, which is the most important to focus on for TODAY's conversation	
	Get them to repeat the problem statement in ONE sentence	
O	• what is your prefferd outcome • what would you like instead • if you had a magic wand, what outcome would you like	
	Your job is to SHIFT the FOCUS from problem to SOLUTION !! **Help them to articulate the Outcome as a SMART Goal**	
	• what is your specific outcome • tell me in one sentence • by when	
	Get them to repeat their OUTCOME as a one sentence SMART Goal	
W	• what is the very next physical action • what else, what else, anything else • what is an action that you've not taken before, that you could take • what would your role model suggest	
	You are supporting your coachee with a mini-brainstorm. Help them prioritise the top 2, then dig deeper	
	• out of these 4-6 actions, which are the two most important • for priority No.1, what specific actions do you need to take, by when	
	Action#1 - by when **Action#2 - by when** **Action#3 - by when**	

Sometimes, during your early coaching practice, you may be running out of time during your conversation. Initially, allocate thirty minutes for your conversation, and after a month or so of practice, twenty minutes will be enough.

Whatever amount of time you allocate, you're eventually going to have the challenge of running out of time. You might feel like you're just a few minutes into the Way Forward, and you notice the time. Either you or your coachee has another meeting or appointment afterward, so you don't have any extra time to fully complete the process.

There are a couple of questions and strategies you can utilize if this is the case. For example, you glance at your watch and phone and notice you only have three to five minutes remaining. A few example questions to cleanly wrap up the conversation in the limited time you have remaining:

- OK, we've got just a few minutes remaining, please tell me your No.1 priority (allow them to share, then follow with), and what do you need to do specifically, to complete that, and by when?
- OK, we've got just a few minutes left before your next meeting, what is your first specific action (let them share), and your second?
- Wow, just two minutes left before we need to leave, please tell me quickly, your top two actions, and by when
- OK, in the couple of minutes remaining, kindly summarise your top two actions as quickly as you can

Ultimately, you want to elicit at least two or three very clear, specific, and time-based actions. If you've helped them to do that, then they are a few steps closer to instant impact, and achieving their goal.

If there seems to be a lot more to still unpack, get those couple of actions, and then do your best to get their commitment for another conversation, in the near future:

- Great, those actions are clear. Great job. You mentioned a few other topics during our conversation today, would you like to schedule another catch-up later this week or next?
- I'm available any time if you'd like to discuss this further/in more detail. Just send me your availability/use this calendar link, and we'll find a convenient time

You may also gently 'interrupt' them at any point during the POW process if you feel they are taking too long or going off-topic. This is not rude, it's respecting their time, and the process, for the best results.

At its most fundamental, the POW Coaching Model can be summarised as:

Supporting a coachee to focus on what they want, and helping them commit to taking two to three actions to achieve it

Let's break that down a little further...

Supporting a coachee to focus on what they want – this is first listening to them vent and share about their problems, helping them clarify one problem they wish to solve, and then through the power of asking questions, helping them to shift that focus towards a solution, by supporting them to create a SMART goal.

Helping them commit to two to three actions to achieve – there is NO other way to achieve a goal, except through action. Once that SMART Goal is clear, you must help them get as detailed as possible, on WHAT actions they will take, and BY WHEN they will take those actions. As we help them break it down into the very next physical action, they are much more likely to take those actions (when you're not around) and move closer to the achievement of their goal.

Simplified further ... elicit their goal and elicit their actions. That's it.

To watch a few demonstrations of real-life POW Coaching conversations, please scan the QR code below, to observe the full process. You will notice that every conversation is different and unique, yet they follow the POW structure very well. All your coaching conversations will also be unique, so it's important to move at the pace of your coachee, and focus on eliciting their goal, and their actions

Congratulations!! You've now experienced the full POW Coaching Model process. Let's explore some real-life applications, for Instant Impact and best results, using the POW Coaching Model

Awareness and Action: Practice the full POW Coaching Model with at least three different people

CHAPTER 10
Practical POW Coaching Applications

"Being practical is more important than being positive"
– True Living

There are many scenarios and opportunities where the POW Coaching Model is a good match. Summarised here, they are:

- When people come to you with problems
- Problem Solving/Action planning sessions
- KPI development
- Project work
- Performance reviews/pit stops/1-on-1's
- Delivering Feedback

Let's look at each of these in more detail.

When people come to you with problems - Probably the easiest and most organic way to begin utilizing the power of the POW Coaching Model is when your subordinates, peers, or friends come to you with their problems.

A quick glance at your watch will guide you on whether it's a good time. If you can allocate ten to twenty minutes, then go for it. That small investment of time will be returned to you as an amazing

ROI of extra time you'll have in the future. If you know you are really strapped for time, then you can utilize a pre-frame, which is simply sharing your expectations in advance, that you don't have much time.

For example, if one of your team comes to you with a problem, you quickly glance at your watch and see you have twelve minutes before your next meeting, you could then reply:

> "Great, thanks for sharing. I've got a full ten minutes, tell me more…"

> "Thanks for bringing that to my attention. We've got ten minutes, let's dive in, and please summarise the situation in one sentence…"
> "OK, we have ten minutes max, the challenge is clear, tell me your preferred outcome…"
> "Great, clear. In the three minutes remaining, please tell me the top two actions you can take"

These statements and questions will help keep your coachee focused, will allow you to speed up the pace a little, and will be an excellent and efficient use of everyone's time.

When you glance at your watch and you can see you really don't have the time, you could simply schedule a time for later in the day when you're free, such as:

> "Thanks for bringing that to my attention. I'd love to give it the time it deserves, to explore fully. Are you available at 3pm to discuss this in more detail?"

A quick reminder here that TELLING your team how to solve their problem is NOT coaching. It's our natural tendency, and if we continue to keep telling them, we are not helping them to solve their own problems, and we are not empowering them to the next level. Yes, it may seem quicker to tell them what to do, so we must also remind ourselves that any time invested in coaching, we will receive a massive ROI of that time.

Many times, when the coachee presents you with the problem, that problem statement is very clear and obvious, so you don't need to spend much time on that, enabling you to get clear on their outcome and actions, more quickly.

Problem Solving/Action planning sessions – this will typically be in group sessions or team sessions, and the POW Coaching Model works equally as well with groups as it does with individuals. You'll simply follow the exact same POW model, with the group. It may take slightly longer, as you need to ensure all the team is aligned with each step of the process. Allow yourself at least 30min to complete a session fully, when working with a group.

When working with groups, you may choose to extend the Way Forward process, into a fully developed action plan. You should still highlight those very next physical actions, and you can also arrange the mid and longer-term actions, into a consolidated action plan. This will extend the process to approx. 45 minutes. The advantage of a larger group is that the actions can be shared around and delegated to more people, so more actions are being taken, and that initial 'problem' is being solved more quickly

If it's a larger group, say 12+, then it might be best to split it out into smaller groups. You could have the separate groups work on the same problem/outcome/actions and see what each group comes up with. If multiple problems/challenges are going on, have one group focus on one challenge, and other groups focus on other challenges. This is an excellent use of time. And you, as the Coach and Facilitator, simply guide them through the process, each step of the way. This can be facilitated traditionally, in some kind of training or meeting room, using flip charts and markers, or you can facilitate the same sessions virtually, which was the norm for a couple of years, during lockdowns and covid.

KPI Development – typically, individuals within an organization, whether they are an individual contributor or part of a larger team, will utilize Key Performance Indicators, or KPIs, to measure the effectiveness and productivity, within their role. Some typical KPIs might be:

- $50,000 in sales per month – for someone in Sales
- 95% customer satisfaction each month – for someone in Customer Service
- 1,000 website clicks per month – for someone in Marketing
- 8% profit for the fiscal year – for the MD/GM
- 35,000 units produced per week – for someone in Manufacturing
- Salaries accurately paid on time within the 27th of each month – for someone in HR

While the KPI may seem obvious, in these above examples, many employees have multiple KPIs tied to their performance criteria. Achievement or non-achievement of these KPIs is often reflected in whether or not they receive bonuses or salary increases.

Even though the KPI itself is relatively easy to understand, the exact process of HOW to achieve them is not so clear. That makes it a perfect opportunity to coach that person, to first help them articulate their SMART goal, followed by their Way Forward on how to achieve it. As months go by, if they have any 'problem' of not achieving their KPI, then you can dig down deeper, to create sub-goals, milestones, and different actions to help them achieve it.

By coaching them through this process, you are helping them take greater responsibility and accountability, for their own KPIs

Project work – any form of project work, big or small, easy or complicated, is another excellent opportunity to utilize the POW Coaching Model. Again, you can work with individual stakeholders working within the project, or, as a sub-group or larger group. The exact same principles apply, and typically, a project may be slightly more complicated, as many tasks are happening in parallel, at the same time, and other times, one step of the project needs to complete before another step can begin.

Utilizing some kind of Gantt chart or project management software can help keep you on track with the overall project status and timelines. Your job as the Leader is to ensure project success. Checking in with the individual members of the project is a great organic way to implement your coaching skills. Simply asking 'any challenges or concerns' is a great way to get started.

On a monthly or quarterly basis, you could conduct sessions with the larger groups.

Performance reviews/pit stops/1-on-1's – Another great opportunity here to support your team with the benefits of Coaching. Opening the conversation with a focus on what has been working well, their success, and wins, is a great way to keep the energy up. Following the principles of coaching, you can then ASK them questions such as:

> "What are some areas you would like to improve"
> "What challenges/problems did you have during the last xx months"
> "What are your professional development goals for the next year"

Questions like this give ownership to the individual, which helps with their responsibility and accountability. As they share those problems or challenges, you simply begin your POW Coaching Model process.

Delivering Feedback – Firstly, please help me to re-brand feedback. Sadly, it has this kind of negative feeling and emotion towards either delivering or receiving feedback. We need to appreciate that feedback is truly a gift. What is the real reason or purpose for delivering feedback? Simply, it's to help the other person improve. That's it!! And that is a positive intention.

Its 'bad' reputation stems from the fact that most Leaders are never taught a practical way to deliver feedback, and when it is delivered, it's often delivered with an emotional 'edge' because we've delayed giving the feedback for so long.

We've already discussed the BIFF Model for delivering effective feedback, and it's the final step – F for Future – where you will begin the POW Coaching Model.

During the first part of BIFF, you are focusing on the problem, which is usually a behaviour or performance issue. That makes the P part of POW, very clear. You will then want that nice transition through to Outcome. When delivering the feedback, you will want to share your clear expectations of the desired performance or behaviour that you want from the individual, so in a certain way, you are helping them (more directly) come up with the Outcome statement. It is a co-creation though, and you will both need to mutually agree on the 'by-when' for the achievement of the Outcome.

Then the magic happens. You now switch into full ASKING mode, as you begin to focus on the actions they need to complete, in the future, to achieve their outcome. This is the time to elicit their actions FROM THEM, with very clear milestones and 'by-whens' for each action.

For example, let's imagine a scenario where Bob has been continually coming late to work, over the last couple of weeks. We'll utilize the BIFF Feedback model, with the transition to the coaching conversation towards the end. It might sound like this:

> Leader: Hey Bob, do you have a few minutes for a straight talk
> (always seek permission first)
> Bob: Yeah, sure boss
>
> Leader: Great, thank you. Bob, I've observed that over the last couple of weeks, you've been twenty minutes late on four occasions
> (this is the observed **Behaviour**, based on facts)
> Bob: Uh huh
>
> Leader: This has a significant impact on the team, as they must fulfil your role, which prevents them from getting on with their own work
> (you're sharing the **Impact** of their Behaviour)
> Bob: Umm, yeah
>
> Leader: This makes me feel frustrated and disappointed, as we've spoken about this three months ago. I'm also concerned that there is something I don't know that I don't know what's going on with you
> (you're sharing your **Feelings** here)
> Bob: Yep

Leader: So, focusing on the **Future**, I'd firstly like to clarify that my expectations are that you are here, at work, at your station, ready to go, by 9am sharp, every day. It's also documented here in your employment contract
(you're sharing your expectations and clear outcome)
So, what needs to happen, for you to be here at work, at 9 am sharp, ready to go
(you've just put your coaching hat on)
Bob: Ummm, well boss, I guess I could set my alarm five-minutes earlier

Leader: OK, what else?
Bob: Ummm, I could ask my wife to check I'm awake

Leader: Anything else?
Bob: Umm, I think that's enough

Leader: Bob, permission to share an observation?
(You'll want to challenge these 'soft' actions)
Bob: Yep

Leader: I am not certain that those actions will guarantee you'll be here at work, on time. Five minutes earlier won't really make a difference, and you don't want to always rely on your wife. What can YOU do to ensure, you'll be here by 9am every day
Bob: Well, I guess I can set my alarm thirty-minutes earlier

Leader: Great, what else?
Bob: I can set a backup alarm on the other side of the bedroom, to force me to get up

Leader: Excellent. What could be one more?
Bob: Well, I normally make the kids lunch in the morning, so I suppose I could do that the night before, and pop them in the fridge

Leader: Nice one. And how will you remind yourself to do those things
Bob: Umm, I can adjust my alarm now

Leader: Great, go ahead (if it takes less than 1min, get them to do it NOW)
Bob: OK, done. And while my phone is out, I've set a reminder for 800pm to make the kids lunch, and I've set another reminder to set up the backup alarm, when I get home
Leader: Excellent. Please give me a quick recap of your actions
Bob: Set alarm thirty-minutes earlier, which is done. Make the kids lunch in the evenings, and set up a backup alarm, which I've set a reminder to do tonight

Leader: That's great Bob, thank you. How do you feel about your actions?
Bob: I feel good, and I'm also sorry about being late. Thanks for helping me get refocused

Leader: My pleasure Bob. Is there any further support you need from me?
Bob, No thanks boss, I'm good

Leader: Great, thanks, Bob. Appreciate your efforts

In the above example, you've combined direct communication in the form of feedback, and you've wrapped up the conversation with some coaching questions to encourage Bob to take ownership of his own actions and results.

You'll also notice that if your coachees actions are a little soft, it's OK to challenge them, supporting them to come up with something that will effectively work.

You can conduct all your feedback sessions like this, whether it's situational feedback (a one-off), a recurring behaviour that needs stronger feedback, or feedback that might be part of their performance review.

With continued practice, your POW Coaching conversations will reduce to ten minutes, and will be able to be conducted conversationally. This means you will not always need the official "let's sit down and have a talk", but instead, have those conversations at the water cooler, coffee machine, or lunch break.

Having said that, in the beginning, we do recommend scheduling regular pitstops or 1-on-1s, with your subordinates, at least once per month. This builds your skills, and more importantly, your team gets accustomed to your new Leadership style. They'll know what to expect, and the process will become more efficient.

Now that we've covered all the practical applications of the POW Coaching Model (there are probably other scenarios where the POW Coaching Model is also very effective, so just try it out), it's now time to address challenges they may arise, as you begin implementing your coaching practice. Let's troubleshoot your POW Coaching Conversations.

Awareness and Action: Practice your full POW Coaching Model in three different scenarios outlined above, and notice which one is more effective for you and your team

Chapter 11
Troubleshooting Your Coaching Conversations

"If something isn't working, don't try harder or do more. Do something different"

— Ramit Sethi

There are a few challenges you might experience, as you begin implementing your Leadership Coaching practice. With continued application, repetition, and practice, you will easily be able to navigate those challenges. To help you on your journey, we'll identify some speed bumps that you might experience so that you can be best prepared for them.

We've already touched on some of these previously, and for clarity, we'll share those challenges below, for each segment of POW, and how you can address the challenge

P = Problem/Challenge Statement

Challenge you face as the Coach	Possible Solution
Coachee talks too much	"Please bottom line the situation for me" "Tell me about the problem in one sentence" "In the interests of time, can you summarise the challenge for me" "And how is that a problem"
Coachee layers multiple problems	"I'm hearing a, b and c, which one is most important to discuss today" "I appreciate they're both important, and which one is most important for today's conversation" "Which one should we focus on, that will have the greatest positive impact" "Thank you for sharing. Which is the most important to explore today"
Coachee seems overwhelmed and unable to express themselves clearly	"Take a breath, and please share the challenge that's causing you the most stress" "What's keeping you awake at night" "Please share anything that's on your mind, this is a safe space"
Coachee is too quiet/not saying much	Build more Rapport!! "Ready when you are.." "Tell me more.." "I know you don't have a 'problem', so is there anything else you'd like to discuss" "This is a co-creation process, please let me know how I can best support you" "Please rest assured this is a safe place, and our conversation remains fully confidential"

The coachee doesn't actually have a challenge/problem	"OK, great. Do you have a focus area for development" "Do you have any area where you'd like to grow or accelerate" "Great. Tell me about your professional development plan"
Coachee totally not engaged/present	Build more Rapport!! "Is there anything on your mind that you'd like to clear before we get started" "Bob, what needs to happen for you to be totally present today" "Bob, kindly send that message, and let me know when you're ready" "What outcome would YOU like to achieve today" "You seem distracted, is there anything on your mind"

O = Outcome/SMART Goal statement

Challenge you face as the Coach	Possible Solution
Coachee talks too much	"Please bottom line your outcome for me" "Tell me about your outcome in one sentence" "In the interests of time, can you summarise your goal for me" "How can you make your outcome shorter and more direct" "OK, that's clear, so tell me in one sentence"

Coachee is not making the Outcome SMART	"What is your specific Outcome" "How will you know if you've achieved it" "What is your measure of success" "Please make it present tense" "By when. What date specifically" "Scale it for me – where are you now 1-10, and where would you like to be" "Is that realistic for you" "How relevant is this goal for you" "Can you use a descriptive word that *means* 8/10 for you"
Coachee seems incongruent or is not OWNING their goal	"Can you please repeat your Outcome" "Repeat it again. Say it louder" "Please stand up, hands out of your pockets, and convince me" "Say it without reading it" "You've mentioned two goals just now. Which one is more important for you to focus on today"
Coachee is too quiet/not saying much	Build more rapport!! "What if you had a magic wand, what would your goal be" "If you could achieve anything, what would it be" "This is YOUR goal. What would bring you joy/happiness/success" "Tell me more about your outcome.." "This is a co-creation process, please let me know how I can best support you" "Please rest assured this is a safe place, and our conversation remains fully confidential"

The coachee wants to jump to the actions	"OK, good. They sound like actions. Before we explore those, can we clearly articulate your outcome"
	"Yes, that's a good action step of HOW you might achieve the goal, and let's get a little clearer first on your specific outcome"
	"OK, let's park those actions for a moment. Please clarify in one sentence, your actual Outcome"
	"Before we get to the HOW, can you please clarify your specific outcome first"
Coachee totally not engaged/present	Build more Rapport!!
	"You seem distracted, is there anything on your mind that you'd like to clear before we continue"
	"Bob, what needs to happen for you to be totally present today"
	"Bob, kindly finish sending that message, and let me know when you're ready to continue"
	"Is now the best time to continue the conversation"

W = Way Forward with next physical Actions

Challenge you face as the Coach	Possible Solution
Coachee talks too much	"In the interests of time, can you share your first, most important action"
	"Oh wow, we've got just a few minutes remaining, please tell me your top 2 actions"
	"OK, that's clear, so what physical action can you take"

	"That all sounds good, and, what specific action can you take within 48hr"
	"Quick Quick, tell me your very next action"
The action step is still too 'big'	"What needs to happen before that"
	"Can that be broken down into smaller sub-steps"
	"What do you need to do, before that"
	"What do you need to do, to 'set that up'"
	"What do you need to do to prepare for that"
	"Any pre-work needs to be done before that"
The action step is too 'vague'	"By when. What date specifically"
	"Can you please summarise your actions steps"
	"HOW will you actually do that"
	"OK, so what specific action is that"
	"So what can you DO physically"
	"What/who/when/how specifically.."
	"What can you actually do or delegate here"
Coachee doesn't know what action to take	"What could be one more action"
	"I know you don't know, but if you did know"
	"What is one action you could take, that you've not taken before"
	"What small action could you take, that will inch you one step closer to your goal"
	"What would your role model recommend"
	"What would I recommend you do"
	If they really get stuck, you could ask a leading question, such as

	"Could you speak to someone that could help you"
	"Could you gather a certain group of people to discuss this.."
	If they are still stuck, you can put your 'Mentor' hat on and say:
	"Permission to share an option…What if, you spoke to Mary at accounting"
	"Permission to share a possibility…What if, you arranged a meeting with 'those' people"
The actions are too 'soft'	"What could be another option"
	"What would help shift the needle even more"
	"Are you sure that action will help you achieve your goal"
	"That's one option, what could be a stronger option"
	"What is that one action that you don't want to take, that if you did take, would get you closer to your goal"
	"What if it were easy.."
	"What if anything were possible, what action would you take"
	"Permission to share an observation…I'm not sure that action is 'strong' enough. What else could you do"

Coachee not engaged/ present	Build more Rapport!!
	"We're almost there. Please just share your next one or two actions"
	"Stay with me please Bob, just a few more minutes.."
	"Bob, I know you've got that meeting in just a few minutes, please kindly share your number one action"

These cover most of the challenging behaviours you will experience from your Coachee. Of course, every coachee is different, and they can often be very 'creative' with the resistance that they show. Remember, many times, especially if your coachee is new to coaching, they simply don't know what they don't know. This will take patience and guidance from you (in the form of questions) to help your coachee navigate their uncertainty. Rule number one, to ensure a smoother coaching conversation is build more rapport. That mutual trust and respect is an ongoing process. The more rapport you have, the more instant and impactful the results will be!

Getting Unstuck

The final challenge you may encounter during your coaching conversations, is that your coachee gets stuck, especially on the Way Forward and next physical actions. They've articulated their problem, you've helped them articulate their SMART goal, and you try to elicit some actions, and get that blank stare off into space. They 'search' for something, then finally look at you and say, "I don't know, please tell me". Other ways this shows up is:

- Loooooong silences – generally, you will encounter some silence during your coaching conversations, and this is

a GOOD thing. It means your coachee is thinking new thoughts. However, long pauses and silences could mean they are struggling
- They repat the same actions as before – if their goal is relating to their KPI or performance, then chances are, you've had similar conversations with them before, and they just keep sharing the same old actions (that didn't work before)
- They get emotional – sometimes, they may feel that they are getting backed into a corner, and may react with anger, frustration or tears. Stay focused, and help them come out the other side
- I don't know – they really don't know what action to take

To help you navigate this, we recommend this three-step process for getting your coachee unstuck. Start at Step 1 and keep moving through the steps until they get unstuck:

1. **Keep Asking them questions** – keep asking questions from different perspectives, such as:
   - 'What would I recommend' or
   - 'What if it were easy' or
   - 'I know you don't know, but if you did now'
   and other similar types of questions. Don't give up on them. Be patient, have empathy, and get creative in the questions you ask

2. **Ask them a leading question** – because you want to support them to have instant impact, in the interests of time, and when they are really stuck, gently ask them a leading question that might give them a 'clue' to a potential action. For example:
   - 'Is there someone you could speak to in accounting?'
   - 'Is there some specific research you could do?'

- 'Is there some kind of meeting you could set up?'
  By structuring your questions this way, it supports them to still take ownership of the action they decide, and it speeds up the process

3. **Tell them, with permission** – this is the final resort, if you are really strapped for time, and if they haven't come up with any 'suitable' actions yet. We still want them to 'own' the action, so you can wrap up your suggestion in a question. Also, because you still want to strengthen your coaching skills, we recommend you start with a permission question first:
    - "Permission to share one possibility/option" – wait for the yes, then follow...
    - "What if you spoke with Mary in accounting"
    - "What if you research competitor a and b and see what their marketing/sales strategy is"
    - "What if you scheduled a meeting with a, b and c departments?

    By putting the 'what if...' in the beginning, it's not a command, and they can still own the action, making them more responsible and accountable. Importantly here, when you do give your suggestions, do it in a neutral, non-attached way, and they may not like your suggestions.

    Failing all the above, switch gears to Mentoring mode, tell them what to do, and set your follow up session with them.

Awareness and Action: Try these different questions and strategies with your different coachees, and see which ones work the best for you. Especially those coaches who you feel may be difficult or challenging. Re-read this chapter, directly before your coaching conversation.

Congratulations, you now have all the tools necessary to develop your teams through the power of coaching. We've created a community of like-minded Leaders and Coaches, where we share success stories, ask questions, and continue to learn and grow on our coaching journey. Please join our exclusive POW Coaching group, where you can practice your POW Coaching Conversations, and network with like-minded professionals. Simply scan the below QR code.

CHAPTER 12
Acknowledgments

This little book has been ten years in the making. With stops and starts, changes in direction, and an initial 'larger' book split into three unique Coaching books. None of it would have been possible, if not for the loving support of my Life Partner, Business Partner, and amazing Coach, Cristy Aphimonthol MCC. Our journey together with Coachology has been one of the most unique blessings in my Life. The passion we share for teaching these coaching principles to over one thousand Leaders around the world and hearing the stories of true, long-lasting transformation, fills our hearts with joy. Thank you, Cristy, for your inspiration and for being a role model of what it means to be an amazing Coach.

I've also been blessed with many great Coaches, Mentors, and Leaders in my Life. From the tough love I received from Ole Larson to the silky-smooth Mentoring from Jean-Francois Cousin, every role model I have ever looked up to has shaped me in some positive way.

The forty-five minute coaching conversation I received from Alonzo Cahoon, backstage at a Tony Robbins event truly changed the direction of my Life and helped me unlock power and possibility I'd only ever dreamed of.

My mother, Anne Salway, helped me discover the art of non-judgemental listening and presence. The ability to hold space for another is a true gift, and is something I continue to work on, to better serve my coachees.

My father, Allan Salway, taught me the importance of hard work and integrity. Qualities I learned while working weekends as a teenager, through to my first 'proper' job.

My first real boss, Jan Beunder, who taught me there is a time to work and a time to play. Work hard and play harder has continued to be a motto that guides me to this day

From John Ens, my General Manager at that beautiful boutique resort in Koh Samui Thailand, I learned the power of asking questions and empowering others with decision making.

Thank you to Howard Bryant for your friendship, counsel, and amazing proofreading skills

To all our students, near and far, who placed their trust in us, for their Personal and Professional Development…thank you!! I've learned something from each of you, all of which has made me a better Coach, a better Leader, and a better man.

To our amazing staff and partners at Coachology. Thank you for your feedback, thank you for your agility, and thank you for sharing this amazing journey together.

Thank you to Marshall Goldsmith for being a shining light in the coaching industry.

Thank you to Tony Robbins for showing me how energy and emotional state can positively influence the world around you.

Thank you to Dr. Joe Dispenza for playing an integral role in my inner journey.

Thank you to all the nemeses' that have appeared in my life, and who then magically disappeared, when I learned the lesson that needed to be learned.

And finally, thanks to you, the one reading this. The world is ready for more professional coaches, and we hope that you empower the people you work with, one Leader at a time, helping them to discover Instant Impact!

www.ingramcontent.com/pod-product-compliance
Lightning Source LLC
Chambersburg PA
CBHW051536240526
45465CB00027B/353